VERSES

VERSES

Lola Ridge

with an introduction by Michele Leggott

Quale Press

Acknowledgements: Michele Leggott's introduction first appeared in issue 12 of *Ka Mate Ka Ora: A New Zealand Journal Of Poetry And Poetics*, in March 2013. It is reproduced, with edits, by kind permission of *Ka Mate Ka Ora* and its editor Murray Edmond. Notes on the poems, and the text presented in this edition, are based on the extensive research by Michele Leggott, especially on prior periodical publication of Ridge's poems. Quale Press would also like to acknowledge the assistance of the Mitchell Library of the State Library of New South Wales in Australia. Quale Press would, above all, like to thank Catherine Daly for bringing Ridge's manuscript to the press's attention and for providing the press with a copy of it.

Cover: *Hokitika Township ca. 1870s*, photograph by James Ring, accessed from the Alexander Turnbull Library, National Library of New Zealand, original print reference no. PA7-51-05-1.

ISBN: 978–1–935835–24–0 trade paperback edition

LCCN: 2019930789

Quale Press
www.quale.com

Contents

Verses and Beyond: The Antipodean Poetry of Lola Ridge

Michele Leggott

Sometime between 1902 and 1905 Lola Ridge submitted a manuscript of forty-six poems to A. G. Stephens, literary editor of *The Sydney Bulletin*, who was bringing out books by promising Australian writers under the imprint of the magazine.[1] Ridge published fourteen poems and a short story in the *Bulletin* between October 1901 and February 1905, but she was not Australian and the poems sent to Stephens begin the job of uncovering a trans-Tasman background that is in many ways typical of the era when the West Coast of the South Island of New Zealand was still easier to reach from Melbourne and Sydney than via the transalpine routes across the island from its East Coast. This investigation sets out to find the antipodean poet Lola Ridge and to connect her with the American Modernist Lola Ridge who came to prominence in the late 1910s and early 1920s then faded from view in the 1930s. By the time of her death in New York City in 1941, Ridge's work was thoroughly unfashionable and it is only in the last few years that her story and her poetry have come to light again as literary scholars reassess the contribution of politically engaged writers through the first part of the twentieth century.[2] Scholarship knows a version of Ridge's Australian sojourn, based mostly on what she told early biographers, but we know very little about the New Zealand life and work she left behind in 1903 as she crossed the Tasman and entered the literary and artistic milieu of Sydney. Mobility and determination were Ridge's signatures, and the manuscript of poems that arrived on A. G. Stephens' desk was part of a plan for recognition beyond the confines of New Zealand.[3]

Ireland, Australia, New Zealand, America

white sea foam in the schooner's trail
—"The Last Lover"

Lola Ridge was born Rose Emily Ridge at Dolphin's Barn in Dublin, Ireland, December 12, 1873 and was known variously as Rose, Rosa, Rosalie, Dolores and Lola. The birth certificate lists her father's occupation as "medical student" and from Dublin street directories of the day it would seem that her mother and father, Joseph Henry and Emma Ridge (née Reilly), were living with maternal relatives in the Reilly household at 1 St. James' Terrace when their daughter was born. She was brought to Australia by Emma Ridge in 1877 when she was three years old. Nothing more is heard of Joseph Henry Ridge, nor is it clear when mother and daughter travelled on to New Zealand. The solo Mrs. Ridge had a married sister in Australia and married again herself when she reached New Zealand; her new partner was a miner named Donald McFarlane. They were married in September 1880 in Hokitika on the West Coast of the South Island and Rose Emily, now known as Rosalie McFarlane, grew up on the nearby goldfields that were the reason for the town's existence. She wrote and painted (there are poems published in local newspapers from 1892), and was almost twenty-two when she married Peter Webster on December 6, 1895 at the house of Mrs. D. McFarlane in Hokitika. The bride, whose present and usual residence was given as Hokitika, described herself as a painter. The groom was a twenty-five-year-old miner, born in nearby Kaniere and resident in Kaniere Forks, a mining settlement some eight miles southeast of Hokitika. His father was James Webster, also a miner, and his mother was Margaret (née Sanderson). Kaniere, about four miles from Hokitika along the river, had been one of the richest West Coast goldfields of the mid-1860s.

Electoral rolls and post office directories show that Peter and Rosalie Webster lived at Kaniere Forks, and the poems of the typescript sent to Stephens reference Hokitika, Kaniere Forks and environs. A first child, Paul, was born on December 9, 1896 and died two weeks later of bronchitis; a second, Keith, was born on January 21, 1900. At some point the marriage foundered. Rose Webster left the West Coast of New Zealand and went with her mother and surviving son to Sydney, arriving from Wellington on November 11, 1903 by the *S.S. Mokoia*. Soon the little family was living on Sydney's North Shore and Ridge told Stephens that she was studying art and working at the Julian Ashton Academy in the city. An annotation in Stephens' hand reads: "Asked for her married name to be omitted," which was not an unusual request at a time when pen-names and pseudonymity were prevalent. Ridge continued to write and publish in her new surroundings. Australasian bibliographical sources show that she published mostly as "Lola" until late 1902 and as "Lola Ridge" from April 1903, but she was known as Rose or Rosa

Webster to her editors. There are poems and prose indexed under Ridge and Webster, but with the exception of one author-illustrated short story and a small number of drawings, records of painting or illustrative work from the period have yet to be retrieved.[4]

Ridge left Sydney and the southern hemisphere for good in 1907 when she embarked for the North American West Coast shortly after the death of her mother, aged seventy-four, on August 2 of that year. She took her seven-year-old son with her, travelled under an assumed name and subtracted ten years from her age on arrival in California. Rose and Keith Webster disappeared as the San Francisco *Overland Monthly* of March 1908 introduced "Lola Ridge, a young Australian poet and artist, who is not without fame in her own land." By late 1908 Ridge was in New York, settling into Greenwich Village, and beginning an American career that combined anarcho-feminist politics and an interest in educational reform on the one hand with free verse aesthetics and an increasingly mystical utopianism on the other. She knew and admired Emma Goldman and Alexander Berkman, designing a cover for Goldman's 1908 pamphlet *Patriotism: A Menace to Liberty* and contributing twice (in 1909 and 1911) to the radical monthly *Mother Earth*. She was an early supporter of the Communist revolution in Russia, published frequently in *The New Republic* and was arrested in 1927 with other literary figures protesting the execution of anarchists Sacco and Vanzetti in Boston. Ridge joined the New York Ferrer Association as it was formed in 1910 and edited the first issue of *The Modern School*, a journal dedicated to educational reforms advocated by Francisco Ferrer, a Catalan radical executed in 1909 by Spanish authorities fearful of the influence his unconventional Escuela Moderna was spreading in Barcelona.

Lola Ridge met fellow free-thinker David Lawson (1886–1980) at the Ferrer Association in 1910. The couple left New York City in 1912 and lived variously in upstate

New York, Pennsylvania, Ohio and Missouri, settling also for a time in New Orleans and moving to Detroit in 1915. In September 1917, Ridge returned to New York; Lawson followed in December and they were married on October 22, 1919. Lawson records that when he and Ridge reached New Orleans on their southern travels they sent for Lola's son, who was living out West.[5] This is a rare public mention of the erstwhile Keith Webster, who would then have been in his early teens.[6]

Sometime between 1913 and 1917 Ridge encountered Imagist poetics and made them her own, anticipating by a decade or so the blend with Leftist politics that produced Objectivist writing in the late 1920s. In 1918, after the five-year absence from New York that is also the timeframe for her adoption of Imagist techniques, she published "The Ghetto," a free verse sequence about conditions on the Lower East Side in the Hester Street Jewish community. It was the title poem of the collection published that year and led to appearances in Harriet Monroe's *Poetry* (Chicago) and Alfred Kreymborg's *Others* magazine. *The Ghetto and Other Poems*[7] is the work for which Ridge is primarily remembered, but it is her second book, *Sun-Up and Other Poems*, published in 1920 and also from the radical publisher B. W. Huebsch, that concerns us here.[8] Its title poem, another free verse sequence, is a vivid evocation of the years between three and, perhaps, six of a child who crosses the ocean with her mother to begin a new life in an unnamed but clearly antipodean setting.

I read "Sun-Up" trying to determine whether it was Hokitika's sandhills the child was looking at, or some location on Sydney's North Shore. Snakes and bluegums tip the balance in favor of Australia, but it is worth noting that the world of the poem is unconcerned with names; it creates a child's consciousness and the beginnings of a poet's cosmogony. It is also a tour de force and in New Zealand it needs to stand alongside Ursula Bethell's sequence of poems "By the

River Ashley," the poetic prose of Katherine Mansfield's "Prelude," "At the Bay" and "The Doll's House" and Robin Hyde's sequence "Houses by the Sea." All were composed in the 1920s and 1930s; all recreate childhood experience in modes the adult woman artist develops decades after the narrative time evoked, letting us in on history that is about remembering what has been forgotten or dismissed. Bethell's 1870s and 1880s, like Ridge's, escape Victorian rigidities; Mansfield's 1890s glow with empathetic detail; Hyde's 1910s are gritty and difficult. We listen and we recognize the psychological portraiture being undertaken, as when Ridge's protagonist in "Sun-Up" constructs a view of heaven and hell from the world in front of her and its interlocutions with a life of the imagination:

> You can see the sandhills from our new room.
> Butterflies
> live in the sandhills
> and lizards
> and centipedes.
> If you keep very still
> lizards will think you a stone
> and run over your lap.
> Butterflies' liveries
> are scarlet and black.
> They drive chariots in air.
> People in the chariots
> are pale as dew—
> you can see right through them—
> but the chariots
> are made of gold of the sun.
> They go up to heaven
> and never catch fire.
> There are green centipedes
> and brown centipedes

and black centipedes,
because green and brown and black
are the colors in hell's flag.
Centipedes
have hundreds of feet
because it is so far from hell
to come up for air.
Centipedes
do not hurry.
They are waiting for the last day
when they will creep over the false prophets
who will have their hands tied.

At the end of the poem, the authoring child constructs but also deconstructs, and learns that the world may delete a treasure:

Mama never knew about Jude.
You always wanted to tell her,
but somehow you never did.
You were afraid she'd smile
and say he wasn't real—
that he was only a little dream-boy,
because the grass didn't fall down under his feet. . . .
He is fading now. . . .
He is just lines. . . like a drawing. . . .
You can see mama in between.
When she moves
she rubs some of him out.

But "Sun-Up," triumph of the new modes though it is, also points back at the selection sent to A. G. Stephens and headed up "Verses by Lola Ridge." The buried antipodean history beyond the carefully lensed childhood of "Sun-Up" is on view in *Verses* and no less interesting for being in metrical, rhyming forms. Ridge's practice is as good as that of her *Bulletin* peers, and better than many local examples in the newspapers of the day either side of the Tasman.

The Typescript in the Mitchell Library

> . . . *sun*
> *spurting up gold*
> *over Sydney, smoke-pale, rising out of the bay*
> —"The Dream," *Sun-Up and Other Poems*

The poems Ridge submitted to Stephens were probably holographs and it was Stephens who had them typed up as a ninety-three-page blueprint for a collection. He was also responsible for the functional but unexciting title under which they appear. A contents list was typed, complete with page numbers and alphabetized by title. It shows that Stephens included revisions of two poems sent by Ridge ("The Flame Flower" and "Song of the Earth Spirit") because both versions are present, "Song of the Earth Spirit" with this typed note below its typed signature: "I revised these pieces last night & as they seem to sound better am sending you the copy."

It is a nice touch to hear the poet's conversational voice suddenly through the transcription of the typist, and to realize that the selection was being taken seriously by both Stephens and Ridge. But transcription also raises the question of responsibility for the significant levels of error in the typescript. Was Ridge's handwriting bad? (For example, the typescript has *moka* for *smoke*, *Dolorias* for *Dolores*, *premanted* for *supplanted*). Is her spelling indifferent or is the typist in error? (*Flys, skys, mistical, rythm, spangel, gallexys*.) The typist was following closely an instruction to reproduce everything on the original pages. S/he transcribed as interlinear information what must have been watermarks on some of Ridge's stationery: several manufacturers' marks of the British paper-making company H. M. Greville are noted as if they are part of the poem in which the watermark appears.[9] Someone, probably Stephens, has scored out the intrusions and left other corrections in the text as well as a pencil note on the title page under Lola Ridge's name: "Born Dublin, Ireland, 1876 / Came to N.Z. as a child / Three of following pieces / published in *Bulletin* / Others unpublished / —never collected." A short distance below is a fainter annotation: "April 1905."

It looks as if the poems were on Stephens' desk a long time if we take the first part of the note at face value because Ridge's third *Bulletin* publication was "The Three Little Children" (March 15, 1902) when she was still signing herself "Lola" and still resident in New Zealand. The two earlier contributions, also narrative ballads, were "A Deserted Diggings: Maoriland" and "By the Mouth of the Shaft"; both appeared in a section of the *Bulletin* called "Bards from the Backblocks." It is possible that three years passed between the original manuscript submission and the annotation "April 1905" on the typed up poems, and we should remember that Ridge was a recent arrival on Stephens' horizon as he weighed up the chances of book publication.

Alfred George Stephens selected and edited eleven volumes of poetry and two anthologies in his capacity as head of the *Bulletin*'s book publishing department between 1897 and 1905,[10] but he did not publish Lola Ridge's *Verses* though more than half its contents appeared in the *Bulletin* between 1901 and 1907. It is tempting to think that Stephens backed off because Ridge was too junior to be worth a book in 1905, rather than because her poetry was insufficiently Australian in its markings. He was after all an exceptional advocate of Australasian writing at a time when it seemed likely that New Zealand would join Australia as a seventh state in the Federation of 1901. During Stephens' *Bulletin* editorship the proportion of New Zealand contributors increased dramatically and among his papers is a list of 172 authors and artists of Australia and New Zealand with place and date of birth and working pseudonyms, and a compilation of "Austrazealand Pen-Names, 1890–1925."[11] Lola Ridge appears in the latter and her 1904 letter to Stephens is filed in yet another list, "Autobiographies of 231 Australian and New Zealand Authors and Artists, 1901–1924."[12]

The proposed volume does not hide its origins, though its west-facing, trans-Tasman character is also pronounced and Ridge's own nomadic history is present in its trajectories. It is not possible to tell who ordered the poems, though Stephens seems to have added the two revisions as the manuscript was typed. The structure of the typescript is coherent and whoever devised it had a clear idea of what the volume represented. From personal lyrics to public address, genre romance, idiosyncratic mythography, station verses and gold mining ballads, "Verses by Lola Ridge" is a book of predominantly New Zealand poems.

Or rather, it is a work in progress; one stage of the journey caught by the archive as a carbon typescript in Stephens' papers. For there was a second typescript that was in the possession of Ridge's Australian relatives for many years before its disappearance in the 1980s. It too was entitled *Verses* and dated April 1905, but it contained four more poems than the first typescript and was a later compilation, incorporating handwritten corrections from the earlier document and including only the revised version of "The Flame Flower." The second typescript was a top copy, typed on a different machine but its connections with Stephens' typescript were close and it provided confirmation that the volume was retyped at least once more by someone in the *Bulletin* office.[13]

Stephens too was on the move in the second half of the decade; he left his *Bulletin* position in October 1906 to set up as an independent literary agent and publisher. When the venture failed he took a job on the *Wellington Evening Post* in 1907, returning to Australia in 1909. Nothing further came of his Ridge typescript. The annotated carbon was eventually bound with two works by John Neilson and his more famous son John Shaw Neilson, a poet whom Stephens published in 1919 as Ridge was achieving her American breakthrough. All three typescripts are entitled *Verses* and are uniform in their appearance: title page with biographical and publishing notes, alphabetized list of contents, holograph corrections and other editorial marks throughout. They are part of a sequence of manuscript and typescript volumes now in Stephens' papers at the Mitchell Library in Sydney.

Love and Pain

the hot sky flames above the bush-line dim
—"At Sundown," *Bulletin*, Sept. 10, 1903

Traversing the 1905 typescript reveals a sense of location that is crucial to Ridge's early poetics and the journey can be made using some excellent cross-references. The forty-three poems and three pieces of prose published between 1892 and 1908 in the *Bulletin*, *The Canterbury Times*, *The Otago Witness*, *The New Zealand Illustrated Magazine*, *The Australian Town and Country Journal*, *The Lone Hand* and *The Overland Monthly* provide *Verses* with a generous sample of textual variation. Whether the published versions are earlier or later than their typescript cousins does not matter so much as being able to look at the differences between presentation for publication and what editors actually did with the work. Beyond the Australasian publication lies the poet's American oeuvre, five published collections and eighty-plus appearances in periodicals and newspapers, a handful of them reprints from New Zealand and Australian sources. It should come as no surprise to find that Ridge's attention to transnational make-over has a textual equivalent. The 1905 typescript confirms that Lola Ridge was a rewriter par excellence with an acute understanding of the operations of time and place on performance. If something could look or sound better, it was revised and sent out into the world again.

Location, then. Lola Ridge's typescript is a textual Google Earth for its day. We come into it and feel the zoom lens adjust, a series of frames over terrain which is both strange and familiar, here and there, now and then. We enter the space of the text that is signaling attention. Forget (but remember) distances, stand in the Kaniere valley on a summer evening and look west. Her poem "At Sun-Down" (on page 5) brings everything into sharp focus.

This is the ground zero of Lola Ridge's early poetry, a textual and imaginative act underwritten by a sequence of geographical particulars. Stand here and everything fits into place. No need to explain that the pines on the ridge are kahikatea and that it is Melbourne and Sydney the speaker can "hear" in the boom of surf on the infamous Hokitika bar. No need to explain the congruence of red sky and flowering rātā because the emotional correlatives are clear. The flats and terraces of the river valley occur in other poems ("Dead-Pine Shadows" and "To an Old Playfellow") and strong Coast weather delays a lover's arrival from the bush:

> I await you: hath the rain-drift,
>> Sweeping fiercely from the sea,
> Met you out across the plain-drift—
>> Barred you, blown you back from me?
>> —"Waiting," *Bulletin*, Jan. 28, 1904[14]

Other poems at the beginning of *Verses* lose no time putting the eastern sky-line on view ("Dawn on the Mountains" and "The Hour of Dawn") and establishing the mix of grimness and compassion the land seems to offer those who listen ("Under Song" and "The Bush"). The mountain Tūhua and the lake which feeds the Kaniere River are mentioned in

"A Song of the Hills" and become the setting for a tempo-
rary bargain struck between body and solitary poetic soul in
"Lake Kanieri." Looking further, a range of characters peo-
ple the poems, some of them individualized like the invalid
Alice, in the poem "The Incurable," blonde and beautiful on
her crutches in a hospital ward, with only the "dead-house"
to look forward to: "She touches the band of my ring; //
'I'll never wear one on my finger— / Not that it will mat-
ter for much!'" Other figures play out community narratives
of pathos ("The Three Little Children" and "By the Mouth
of the Shaft"), of lurid romance ("When the Moon Was in
Eclipse," "The Flame Flower" and "The Last Lover") or of
vaudeville comedy ("Helblatavesky's Cow," "Laura's Holiday"
and "The Chronicles of Sandy Gully as Kept by Skiting Bill").
Nobody in the poems is specifically identifiable but a strong
impression emerges that any or all of their stories could be
found by reading back numbers of *The West Coast Times*, *The
Grey River Argus*—or for that matter *The Geelong Advertiser*,
The Ballarat Times and *The Armidale Express*.

The geo-historical coordinates of Ridge's poems add
resonance when recognizable but they are in no way limit-
ing when they are not. At their broadest reach they become
freely Australasian—sheep run, country town or gold mine
either side of the Tasman—exemplified by the deletion of
"Maoriland" from the title of "A Deserted Diggings" for its
appearance in the typescript. At their most specific, there are
pleasures to be had on a sliding scale of local knowledge, as
in "The Chronicles of Sandy Gully as Kept by Skiting Bill."
When S. P. Snares, self-styled mining expert from the city
with oiled hair and a forty acre shirt front, decrees that Bill
and Sam's doctored claim is to be floated in a company called
Te Katipō Extended, his partners still think they are in charge
of the webs of deceit. They take Snares' word for it that the
katipō is just "a little spider that does a little weave." Which it
is but if he had called it a redback instead, the partners might

have realized they were up against a master weaver with a lethal bite. *Makes a small sticky web to snare beetles and other crawling insects,* as the identification guide says, extending the fun to be had with the poem's inferences about the ignorance of Australian diggers.[15]

What is to be seen of Lola Ridge's own history in *Verses?* Let's call it autography, the writing of a self or a series of selves, a term that foregrounds construction. Following hard on the conundrum of the bush cloister in "At Sun-Down" comes "On the Track." It remembers a lovers' fight ("Oh! grey were the great bush spaces, / That flung us our wild words back.") and the parting that followed: "I laughed when I heard you sigh it— / 'Good-by,' but no word I said, / The blood in my veins ran riot; / I stayed not your parting tread." Back in town and unable to sleep, the speaker watches breakers scythe onto a shaven beach and excoriates sunbeams because they once shimmered off a tangle of cones caught in her unbound hair. (The *Bulletin* version is more explicit: "For what is their tinsel spangle / To the molten gold they were? / When you strove with the twisted tangle / Of pine-cones in my hair?"). A painful dream of meeting and passing without a word on the sunlit track "known to two" is the poem's final torment. It is neatly replayed by the short piece that was Ridge's next contribution to the *Bulletin* three weeks later:

Love and Pain

Know ye not my name is Pain?
    I am Love's twin brother.
No art o' thine can break the chain
    That binds us to each other.

I let my brother lead the way,
    And then his keys I borrow;

Fond heart, you oped to Love to-day,
You ope to Pain to-morrow!
—*Bulletin*, Oct. 22, 1903

An author is not usually in charge of the order (or timing) of magazine appearances, so the soap-operatic trail of Ridge's poems through the *Bulletin* September–October 1903 may be coincidental. But the same knot of romantic agony is orchestrated in *Verses*: after "On the Track" in the typescript comes "In the Shadow," where the speaker has given everything for love, forgetting even "the voices calling— / Calling to me through the air, / For the warm clasp of your fingers, / And your lips upon my hair." She continues: "I forgot the pride of lineage, / I forsook the hope of fame— / I'd ha' left the road to heaven / For the magic of your name." How literally to read implied detail through dramatic convention? According to her New Zealand marriage certificate Ridge's father was a doctor, and plenty of lineal pride seems to have been invoked over the years to cope with the circumstances she and her mother found themselves in after leaving Dublin. Now it seems that being buried in the bush is too high a price to pay for acquiring the beloved's name when "lips are turned away" and eyes grow "cold & callous." He stands accused of not understanding the depth of her love: "If you loved but as the many, / And my soul you never knew; / All my very life & being / Was but one long thought of you."

In the narrative sequence of the typescript the speaker leaves, and sends back a version of leaving entitled "Think of Me Not With Sadness." But here we will take the *Bulletin* version because it was published a year after the date on the title page of the *Verses* typescript, by which time Ridge had remodeled and retitled the poem as a dialogue, doubling the length of the lines, adding speaker identification and an antiphon in which the deserted one is given a voice:

xxiii

Parted

THE WOMAN:
Oh, think of me not with sad thoughts bedecked in
       mourning grey,
But weave ye a woof about me of colors gold and gay;
For if I were all your own, love, we might regret some day.

Streams at their source united have yet diverging flowed,
And mine is the twisted pathway and yours the trampled
       road:
Who follows uncharted ways, love, alone must bear the load.

In dreaming of me say never— "Her love was false and vain
As cloud of a crimson dawning that falls at noon in rain,
As light of a luring mirage that pales upon the plain."

Think of me with the forest when o'er its ways you see
The sun on the sombre cedars, and flash of bird and bee,
All things that are pure and bright, love, mix with your
       thoughts of me.

THE MAN:
I dream of you—'tis sundown, and low a late bird calls;
A slender moon is pacing beyond the forest walls,
And loud amid its boulders the brawling river falls.

I think of you—not sadly, yet with a half-regret,
As of a song remembered whose rhythm haunts me yet—
As of a fairy legend I cannot quite forget;

Your face against the twilight in dusky shadow lies,
And o'er the bush behind her, where home a late bird flies,
A few white stars are shining as cold as wise men's eyes.
            —*Bulletin*, Apr. 19, 1906

She is figurative, ingenuous (this does not change from the typescript version); he is measured, cool, wounds (almost) covered over. The poem ties off the story of separation symmetrically, leaving layers of submerged conflict available for analysis in the two speaking positions. In its remodeled form the dialogue is a variation on the old discourse of body and soul that Mansfield and Hyde, among others, reinvented as a complex, sexualized contamination of each other by the binary pair, forever unfinished and unwinnable. The 1906 Ridge acknowledges this with greater sophistication than her 1902–05 counterpart—or perhaps the strategies of provocation are simply different. *Verses* offers by one turn of a typescript page after "Think of Me Not With Sadness" the pointed contrast of an address to a childhood comrade from what sounds like the same bush location. "To an Old Playfellow" (on page 20) is detailed and enchanting in its carefully judged nostalgia.

This is a different configuration of high road and low road from the one proffered to the lover left behind in the bush ("Be mine the twisted pathway, / And yours the trampled road"). Has she mistaken kahikatea for kauri, which does not occur naturally on the West Coast of New Zealand; or is kauri an easier word to scan? Otherwise her presentation of indigenous flora and fauna is flawless: the parrots are kākā, the locusts kihikihi (cicada) and the rushes probably raupō. Rātā, tutu, supplejack, tūī and miro are all recognizable components of the surrounding bush. Mica and quartz glint in the gold-bearing creeks of the valley where the noise of mining machinery will resound. The Bunyip stone is an interesting piece of Australian cross-over, maybe the legacy of diggers from Victoria and New South Wales who named such features as Ballarat Hill and Lake Mudgie in the vicinity of Kaniere and Waimea.[16] The "great Bush Spirit" who must be in this context Tāne, supreme god of the forest, also sounds Australian. Ridge's knowledge of the Māori tenure of Aotearoa was good enough to reference a

Percy Smith–based version of the early Polynesian navigator Ui-te-Rangiora, "with his canoe of dead men's bones," in her essay about the differences between New Zealand and Australian bush.[17] But perhaps there are times, culturally as well as metrically, when it is expedient to use an Austrazealand register. "Bunyip" does more to signify watery cryptids than taniwha (*water dragon*, guardian of river bends), and it is the conjuring of shared and remembered dread the poet is nosing out beneath the sunny surfaces of the poem. Like the venomous katipō invoked by S. P. Snares in "The Chronicles of Sandy Gully as Kept by Skiting Bill," the local alert in this poem operates by means of its Māori name. The cue is tutu, fatal to stock (and circus elephants) who chew its new foliage and to humans eating the seeds of its berries. Country children are still taught not to go near it as the berries ripen. The adult speaker is recalling a series of boundary-tests undertaken by the two children, who are portrayed in equal measure as sweethearts and comrades in arms. In addition to making a comparison with the failed marriage, "To an Old Playfellow" should remind us that the unnamed companion is a prototype for the series of playmates reconstructed in "Sun-Up." There are in that poem the sisters Lizzie and Clara, whose names model an enviable and apparently indissoluble bond:

> When it rains
> and you are pulling off flies' legs. . .
> mama lets you play houses
> with Lizzie and Clara.
> Because you are the Only One—
> and because Only Ones have to live alone
> while sisters stay together,
> Lizzie and Clara
> give you the dry house
> and take the one with the leaking roof.

The Only One is attuned to one-on-one bonds, having a life-time monopoly on her mother's attention. It is this she seeks to replicate with another—first the much-beaten doll Janie whom she blindfolds and throws in a ditch, then the white-haired boy Jimmie who shows her startling sexual difference on a dare under the flapping sheets of a neighborhood washing line: "Mabel pulls you in the gate and shakes you / and tells you not to tell your mama. . . / And you wonder / if God has spoiled Jimmie." But the perfect playmate in "Sun-Up" is Jude, red-haired and adventurous, with whom the Only One tries to salvage the drowned doll (no luck) and who shares a secret hut built in a field where the barbed wire is down. Jude deserts when the hideously real boy with a whip and servant appears and claims ownership of the field. By 1920 Ridge knew enough about her relations with the world to allegorize the search for the One and Only who is the Only One's longed-for and beaten-off twin. In *Verses*, the search record is concentrated in the numerous takes on love and rage against self and other that follow on from the poems outlined above. There are plenty of clinging hands and pleading eyes in "My Care," and tumult thrust down "To the padded cell in the soul of me." In "The Parting," rivers will run to mountain tops and the sun stand still before a final farewell is possible; but (next stanza) hell will freeze over before love ignites again in this particular location: "When 'possums mount on moon-shine bars, / And glow-worms hidden in the mine, / Shall leave their caves to mock the stars— / Oh, then my lips shall meet with thine!" There is something refreshing about that gleam of black humor. Not too far ahead of it chronologically is the political bravado of "The Martyrs of Hell" which ends:

> To the Outlawed of men and the Branded,
>   Whether hated or hating they fell,
> I pledge the devoted, red-handed,
>   Unfaltering heroes of hell!
>   —*Mother Earth*, Apr. 1909

Preserve, Renew, Invent

her shut heart closes on its hidden things
—"The Bush," *Bulletin*, Sept. 29, 1904

Location and autography figure strikingly in Ridge's 1905 typescript. The rewriting of remembering may have very short intervals and disclose significant variants, as in the differences between typescript and published versions in the *Bulletin* and other periodicals. Or it may travel the much longer distance between metrical and free verse; more broadly still between nineteenth and twentieth centuries, one life and another. These lines from "The Ghetto"—"And through the uncurtained window / Falls the waste light of stars, / As cold as wise men's eyes. . ."—catapult us from Hester Street back to the imagined nightfall in the bush at Kaniere Forks with the stunning force of repetition and the chasms it opens between one time and place and another. A few lines on in that long poem the young men of the tenements are sleepless in the hot summer night; their minds churn ("Wars, arts, discoveries, rebellions, travails, immolations, cataclysms, hates. . . / Pent in the shut flesh."). They twist on their beds:

And they gaze at the moon—throwing off a faint heat—
The moon, blond and burning, creeping to their cots
Softly, as on naked feet. . .
Lolling on the coverlet. . . like a woman offering her white body.

Nude glory of the moon!
That leaps like an athlete on the bosoms of the young girls
        stripped of their linens;
Stroking their breasts that are smooth and cool as
        mother-of-pearl
Till the nipples tingle and burn as though little lips plucked
      at them.
They shudder and grow faint.

"She is yellow & blond & bare" is the opening line of "Moon-Struck" in *Verses*, spoken by the maddened lover for whom the moon is a faded femme fatale, lolling on a mountain rim and leaving at dawn "With a soul in her strong, white bars, / And a mindless hulk below."

Sometimes the palimpsest takes a less obvious form. "Lake Kanieri" (on page 9) is perhaps the most interesting poem of *Verses* technically speaking because it alone of Ridge's known Australasian work attempts blank verse. An extended metaphor of the beautiful lake as wide-eyed child of its guardian mountain allows the speaker to insert herself on the substitute maternal lap of the lakeshore and hold the world still. Ridge has other peaens to the sublime effects of natural surroundings but nothing quite like this, which sets out to measure (accentually) the systole and diastole of the earth mother. Then it all pours out as the speaker, calmed by the cradling earth, looks again and distinguishes orders of suffering and past upheaval that mirror on a giant scale her own predicament.

The lake is suddenly less anthropomorphic coiling herself for sleep; part of the ultimately inscrutable terrain. The scene is otherwise consistent in its human/inhuman figurations. The dying day is an old man by the embers of his fire. The lower slopes are hooded nuns, the tops a group of stone-faced monks as the light fades. Thirty years later Ursula Bethell, who was also a painter and Ridge's contemporary, observed that the tussocked Cashmere Hills seen in the distance had the texture of paduasoy. Then, because her poem, like Ridge's, lifts off from the prosody and content of Psalm 121 ("I will lift up mine eyes to the hills"), she continues:

> These lines, at night-fall, melting into the arable,
>   Enclosing wine-tawny and grape-violet shades,
> Affect us as a faint air might, played upon a virginal,
>   So long ago that all pain it held then is allayed;

Or clarinet, so far distant it brings us but a memory
   Of healed lament, in the dim twilight dying away.

These hills at dawn are of an austere architecture;
   Claustral; like a grave assembly, night-cold numbed,
Of nuns, singing matins and lauds in perpetuity,
      —Ursula Bethell, "Levavi Oculos"[18]

The powerful image of the nuns appears elsewhere in Ridge's poetry. They, the tired child, the sexual potency of the land and its understanding but hidden heart that must be sought out by the supplicant seem to be rewritten in "Lake Kanieri" from poems such as "At Sun-Down," "Dawn on the Mountains" and "The Bush." All circle parts of the same narrative. "The Bush" calls out to old-timers: "Oh men! heart-tired of unquiet days, / Of sad lives sundered, & strong purpose bent," urging them to share in "the largesse of her clean content." But it is the following stanza that cements the poem emotionally to the meditation beside the lake:

And weary women who have seen love droop
In lust & laughter, till thy bruised hearts yearn,
Some help that stooping shall not seem to stoop,
Seek peace & counsel in her ways of fern.

The dark night of the soul implied in "Lake Kanieri" is picked up across the free verse divide in Ridge's work. The rewrite (or reinterpretation) was published simultaneously in *Poetry* (Chicago) in October 1918 and in *The Ghetto and Other Poems*, and like any variant text elucidates its precursors in the gaps that open between one version of events and another. It seems that the speaker's bid to find peace out on the mountain may have extended beyond finding solace in a sunset. The 1918 repetition puts it like this:

The Edge

I thought to die that night in the solitude where they would
        never find me. . .
But there was time. . .
And I lay quietly on the drawn knees of the mountain,
        staring into the abyss. . .
I do not know how long. . .
I could not count the hours, they ran so fast
Like little bare-foot urchins—shaking my hands away. . .
But I remember
Somewhere water trickled like a thin severed vein. . .
And a wind came out of the grass,
Touching me gently, tentatively, like a paw.

As the night grew
The gray cloud that had covered the sky like sackcloth
Fell in ashen folds about the hills,
Like hooded virgins, pulling their cloaks about them. . .
There must have been a spent moon,
For the Tall One's veil held a shimmer of silver. . .

That too I remember. . .
And the tenderly rocking mountain
Silence
And beating stars. . .

Dawn
Lay like a waxen hand upon the world,
And folded hills
Broke into a sudden wonder of peaks, stemming clear
        and cold,
Till the Tall One bloomed like a lily,
Flecked with sun,

Fine as a golden pollen—
It seemed a wind might blow it from the snow.

I smelled the raw sweet essences of things,
And heard spiders in the leaves
And ticking of little feet,
As tiny creatures came out of their doors
To see God pouring light into his star...

...It seemed life held
No future and no past but this...

And I too got up stiffly from the earth,
And held my heart up like a cup...

Looking back at the cluster of 1905 poems that seem to address parts of the same story, we find an explanation for the strange final stanza of "Dawn on the Mountains" that imagines sunrise as a beautiful dead girl:

Down the day-coast one is borne—
Dawn with golden eyes fast closèd,
And the sun-webs round her drawn—
Dawn with fair white limbs composèd
　　　On the bier of morn.

It is possible, then, to shuttle back and forth between free verse and metrical versions and find ourselves better informed about both? There is one more major nexus, the connection between the lullaby "Sleep Dolores" and the singing mother in "Sun-Up":

Every night
mama sings you to sleep.
When she sings, O for the light of thine eyes Dolores,

there's a castle on a cliff
and the sea roars like lions.
It leaps at the castle
and the cliff knocks it down
but always the sea
shakes its flattened head
and gets up again.
The castle has no roof
so the rain spins silvery webs in it,
and Dolores' face
floats dim and beautiful
the way flowers do when they are drowned.
Step by white step
she goes up the castle stairs,
but the stair goes up into the sky
and the sky keeps going up too,
and none of them ever get there.

The child braids Molly Whuppie–like laterals into the content of the song she is listening to, making the experience ever more fantastic as she drifts towards sleep. The mother's singing takes the same direction as the stairs of the castle with no roof, "and when she has finished singing / her song goes up off the earth, / higher and higher. . . / till it is only as big as a tiny silver bird / with nothing but moonlight around it." The singing storytelling is important in "Sun-Up" and no less so in some of the fables from *Verses* and the *Bulletin* which feature the same straying and often moonlit (or moonstruck) characters. But what, exactly, was in the Dolores song?

The earlier poems supply a darker version of the protective, prescient maternal charm as noted in "'Sleep Dolores'" (page 40):

"Sleep Dolores," my mother sang to me
When Life was like a rose, dear,

Just opening round & red;
Quaint, fantastic, wayward melody—
Now life is dreary prose, dear,
And all its songs are said!

Rose has become prose indeed; the besetting evils of legal and property rights are evidently at the door. Mama's voice comes through the intervening years, sounding an alarm that wakes the daughter to present danger. The song (your mother) will let you go to sleep only as long as the wolves are at a safe distance.

The Legend of the Mother

pale as star-light on a gray wall. . .
—"Mother," *Sun-Up and Other Poems*

Emma Reilly Ridge McFarlane (c1833–1907) must have been a remarkable woman. From public records in Ireland and New South Wales we know that she and her sister Maria (1831–1913) were the daughters of John Reilly, a Collector of Customs, and his wife Maria, née Ormsby. The family seems to have moved about, from Galway where daughters Maria and Emma were born, and perhaps to Drogheda, County Louth, where at the age of twenty-eight Maria married Henry Nicholson Levinge on January 8, 1859. There were no children, and after Levinge's death Maria married again in 1867, this time in Dublin, and had two sons in 1868 and 1870 with Richard Alfred Penfold (c1828–96). Sister Emma was also in Dublin when she married Joseph Henry Ridge in 1871 and would have been about forty in 1873 when Rose Emily was born in Dolphin's Barn at what appears to be the house of her Reilly grandparents. A woman named Sarah Kinsella, of 28 Cole Alley, signed the registration form with an X ("her mark") and was noted as having been present at the birth of Rose Emily Ridge.

The Penfolds emigrated to Australia about 1874, and when circumstances in Dublin changed for Emma Ridge she and her daughter followed Maria, Richard and their two sons to Sydney. "Sun-Up" is elliptic in its coverage of the child protagonist's earliest memories, but in moving from one side of the ocean to another, Betty leaves her beloved Celia (a nursemaid in the household) and goes on a voyage with Mama after the death of her grandfather. Her father is absent, her mother has suffered trauma or illness and the journey itself is compressed into a few lines. In the new place—a city—Mama takes up seamstress work; there is little money and no family save one glimpse of an aunt who is literally the image of the mother: "Mama's face / is smooth and pale as tea-rose leaves. / That ivory oval of aunt Gem / you sucked the miniature off / had black black hair like mama."

We know little about life in Sydney for Emma and Rose Emily Ridge but it seems that the North Shore became family headquarters as the Penfold cousins Richard Alfred and John Edmund Miles grew up, married and had families of their own after the Ridges moved on to New Zealand and Emma's marriage to Donald McFarlane at All Saints Presbyterian Church in Hokitika on September 16, 1880.

It is her second marriage that makes Emma Ridge a real-life Alice Roland (*The Story of a New Zealand River*) arriving in the bush with a young daughter who will grow up socialist and libertarian, disliking her stepfather's line of work while admiring his energy and personal tenacity. Jane Mander's novel, written and published in New York in 1920 and made over by film director Jane Campion as *The Piano* in 1993, is set in the kauri milling districts of Northland in the 1880s and 1890s. It was reviled by local critics for its treatment of sex and religion but well-received in New York and London. Geographically closer still to the Ridges' story is *The Denniston Rose* (2003), a popular novel by Jenny Pattrick about a five-year-old girl (Rose) brought by her mother to the West Coast coal-mining settlement of Denniston in the 1880s. These instances of fictional mother-daughter duos negotiating the conditions of resettlement and (in Mander's book) first-wave feminism in the new land emphasize the importance of recovering the occluded history of both Ridge women. They also contextualize the constructive, autographical achievement of "Sun-Up." The poem leaves us in no doubt about the strength and character of the mother, or her dry humor: "When you tell mama / you are going to do something great / she looks at you / as though you were a window / she were trying to see through, / and says she hopes you will be good / instead of great." *Sun-Up and Other Poems* has a prefatory poem dedicated to the poet's mother and the first poem of its "Portraits" section is entitled "Mother":

> Your love was like moonlight
> turning harsh things to beauty,
> so that little wry souls
> reflecting each other obliquely
> as in cracked mirrors...
> beheld in your luminous spirit
> their own reflection,
> transfigured as in a shining stream,
> and loved you for what they are not.
>
> You are less an image in my mind
> than a luster
> I see you in gleams
> pale as star-light on a gray wall...
> evanescent as the reflection of a white swan
> shimmering in broken water.

The images are allusive, poignant, gesturing at hardship rather than foregrounding it. There is no doubt that life on the West Coast goldfields was tough for all concerned: "A good deal of my childhood was spent in the NZ bush," Ridge wrote in her 1904 biographical note for the *Bulletin*, "In one place I had to walk (daily) ten miles of lonely bush road to school."[19] Later she claimed in a diary written 1940–41 now among her papers at Smith College that the family lived in a three-roomed shack; also that her stepfather was a runaway sailor turned prospector on worked-out diggings who recited Shakespeare to her, told stories from Homer and destroyed the furniture during periodic drunken binges.[20] He was, she noted, the one who comprehended something of the moment one night when she heard in the sound of the running creek outside how poetry was to be made:

> An ache fell on me and I looked at my mother . . . the pure pale cameo of her face—unmoved, disdainfully still sadness . . . she did not hear my waters trebling. [My stepfather], brooding and staring at the log fire [heard nothing], but as though I touched him he glanced up at me . . . [His eyes expressed the defensiveness of a small animal at the mouth of its burrow, his habitual stance. Then his look softened, and he] said in a low grave voice, "I am thinking of my dead sister Jessie." [21]

No age is given but the child is old enough to be working out arithmetic problems in a copybook. After hearing the creek talk, she writes her first poem and shows the page to her mother.

Donald McFarlane (c1832–1906) was born in Scotland, spent forty-two years in New Zealand and was among the earliest miners on the goldfields at Kaniere. He is on Westland Electoral Rolls in the 1890s but his name does not appear on his stepdaughter's marriage certificate as the head of the house where the wedding took place because by 1895 he was an inmate of Seaview Mental Hospital in Hokitika. The asylum records show that McFarlane was diagnosed with symptoms of Mania in late 1894, and after a possibly suicidal episode while on probation he was readmitted to the hospital early in 1895.[22] He remained there ten years, suffering hypochrondriacal delusions according to the Chronic Case Book notes, requiring little or no medical attention and taking an intelligent interest in newspapers and events of the day. The notes also disclose that he went to sea at fourteen and was a sailor for eighteen years. His wife is mentioned once, in 1901, reporting that her husband is still convinced he will commit suicide if released. At the time of his death on January 14, 1906 from pneumonia, she, his stepdaughter and his grandson had been in Sydney for two years, a move which we can view as a return to Penfold family environs.

Lola Ridge's relationship with her stepfather is not manifest in her poems, unless we count some of the generic portraits of miners in the ballads as indicators. More sobering is the evocation of violence, mental and physical, on the goldfield in the melodramatic story "The Trial of Ruth," published 1903 in *The New Zealand Illustrated Magazine* with line drawings by the author. Ruth Dove, dark-haired and pale of face, arresting in her demeanor rather than conventionally pretty, captivates and then marries Paul Sullivan, a lapsed student of law prospecting at Jacob's Flat. Out on the field and living in a two-roomed slab hut, Ruth's happiness implodes as she realizes she has married a drunkard. Complications arise when Sullivan's feckless partner, Harry Dunn, propositions Ruth then takes matters into his own hands by sabotaging the claim in order to remove his rival. A climactic scene involving dynamite, the unconscious Sullivan and Ruth's last-minute dash to pull out the fizzing fuse sees the couple reunited. The treacherous Dunn has taken to his heels, much to the astonishment of Sullivan who cannot understand why his partner has disappeared when their claim is about to pay a handsome return. Ruth keeps her own counsel; her courage and wit have saved the day, her man is reformed ("We'll leave the diggings and open a clean white page in the Book of Love") and the proceeds of the strike are all their own.

Between the lines of Ridge's story we may read something of life with Donald McFarlane in the mining settlement of Kaniere Forks and guess at Emma McFarlane's predicament during the twenty-four years she and her daughter lived in New Zealand. To the child and to the poet she became, her mother was a queen ("[I am] a descendant on my mother's side of a very old Irish race the Princes," she wrote in her 1904 biographical note for the *Bulletin*) and it is not surprising that the poet fashioned a sense of her own legend that was intensely matrifocal. The prefatory poem of *Sun-Up and Other Poems* puts it like this:

Dedication
(To my Mother)

Let me cradle myself back
Into the darkness
Of the half shapes. . .
Of the cauled beginnings. . .
Let me stir the attar of unused air,
Elusive. . . ironically fragrant
As a dead queen's kerchief. . .
Let me blow the dust from off you. . .
Resurrect your breath
Lying limp as a fan
In a dead queen's hand.

Losing Children

The mothers shall reach their kingdom when the sea
hath her own again
—"The Magic Island," *Bulletin*, Dec.14, 1905

Mother. The calling out is preliminary to, but also part of, the authoring construction. You resurrect your mother in the old images of childhood or storytelling, beginning the weave learned as you listened to her voice and made your own visions from what she was saying. Folklore plays its part and perhaps a shared predilection for strongly feminized narrative in keeping with your immediate family situation and (later) the social forces around you that are shaping the late nineteenth-century struggle for the rights of women to educational, economic and political equality.

In *Verses*, the weave of personal and political concerns manifests in poems that work out the speaker's relationship of intimacy and distance with land, sea and sky. As we have seen already, Ridge's universe is animistic, anthropomorphic—and powerfully sexualized. In "The Bush," solar rays penetrate, gullies enfold, the moon is naked and blond, and winds "fondle with the maiden Bush / Who sways & quivers in their close embrace." From "Dawn on the Mountains," sunrise resembles a peepshow: "Light & laughter in the air, / As each roving sunbeam pushes / Prying fingers everywhere; / Eyes obliquely through the bushes / Darting here & there." Sometimes the *Bulletin* editors intervened; "sex & sin" in "Sleep, Dolores" became "shame and sin" and "The Bush" was published one stanza short of its typescript version: "The rival sunbeams their bold fingers thrust / Amid her guarded & most secret sweets; / They steal & nestle on her swelling bust, / And view unchidden all her chaste retreats." That we are looking at editorial rather than authorial revisions seems likely when the same thing happens to "Song of the Earth Spirit," the poem Ridge revised a second time for the typescript. Both typed versions have eight stanzas, but the *Bulletin* publication on November 16, 1905 stops at seven after the Earth's wish for an ocean "To flow over and fondle and fold me / Till our joy be complete." In the omitted last stanza rough play and extra fluids have been excised: "To inundate me, saturate, press me / Over mountain & fen— / Oh arise in your strength & possess me / From the cities of men!" Given the geophysical origins of New Zealand, what the poem has lost is a glimpse of retributive tectonic apocalypse. Earth, weary of the offences of men to her surfaces, wants to go back to the sea. The Tarawera eruption of 1886 is also on view in "Two Nights" but without the eroticized elemental voice present in "Song of the Earth Spirit."

The female sexuality of the planet is nowhere more vividly realized than in the creation stories Ridge invents in two of her longer poems—"The Legend of the Cross" and "The Magic Island." Neither is quite what we might expect from its title, and each is specific to a South Pacific location. *Verses* is curiously devoid of religious poems, apart from pantheistic apostrophes to elemental forces and the occasional, non-denominational call on "God" as an intensifier for strong emotion. Rather than a reworked *Dream of the Rood*, "The Legend of the Cross" delivers a story of earth-sky procreation in which a comet-like star is in love with distantly beautiful Earth ("the dusky maiden"). He travels from beyond the galaxy and falls into her embrace: "Her breasts, two mountains swelling, / Rose soft & round & white, / Her heart's loud clamour quelling / She clasped the son of Light." But he leaves her for the glitter of the Pleiades, speeding off through the Milky Way which is "Hung o'er the roof of heaven / Like nebula of pearls." Earth is desolate: "Dull wak'ning of the 'after' / That she who loves must learn"; she is also pregnant with five star-children. "Sweet Mercy sister Dusk" acts midwife and protector, then more female help arrives:

> And Night the swarthy mother,
> Drew on her sable glove—

Old night the foster Mother,
The screener o' light love!
Where never moon-beam ripples
Down hollow caves she crept,
And from the Earth's warm nipples,
Where clinging still they slept;

She drew each star-child glowing
And dewy from its nest,
The waking eyelids throwing
A halo on her breast;
And covering their faces,
Upon the pale moon bars,
By lone & secret places,
She mounted through the stars.

Night places the babies in the southern sky where Earth watches them open their eyes one by one and grow into the bright guide lights of the Southern Cross. Christianity does not enter into it; this constellation is about a different sacrament of love and loss, with a marked emphasis on midwifery and palliative female wisdom. The poem seems to synthesize Gaia and Uranus with aspects of the primal parents Ranginui and Papatūānuku, whose children were born in the darkness of an embrace that had to be torn apart in order for life to unfold. Contemporary versions of Māori star-lore may also have influenced Ridge's narrative. She does not appear to be remaking any known version of the Polynesian understanding of Māhutonga (Crux), but the five fire children of Mahuika, younger sister of the Dawn Maid, are associated with a comet, Auahi-tūroa ("long smoke") who came to earth bringing fire as a gift.[23] The beauty of Matariki (the Pleiades), whose dawn rising begins the new year in June, may also have been transposed by Ridge: Matariki means "the small eyes"—and Crux is the smallest constellation in the sky. Elsewhere in *Verses* it embodies protection for those who love outside convention ("When the Moon Was in Eclipse") and its implied paradoxes of agony and ecstasy are those of a Storm Fiend urging an abject speaker to "Take up the cross of the longing & loss" and make art like the great souls of the past. Is it because "The Storm Spirit" comes half a dozen poems after "The Legend of the Cross" in *Verses* that some muted personal undertones of longing and loss seem apparent?

Here we might recall the only untitled poem (*"Forgive dear heart. . ."*) in *Verses* contains a crying out to some beloved presence. When the poem was published on July 26, 1905 in *The Australian Town and Country Journal* it appeared without the first stanza and under the title "Beth." Child? Lover? Friend? The same referent as its typescript version or remodeled to fit later circumstance? The specifics are unidentifiable but the pattern of agonized repression is familiar from many of the personal poems of *Verses*.

"The Magic Island" is another synthesized creation story. Its internal referents and its position as the final poem in the typescript identify the island as a version of Aotearoa, but not Te-ika-a-Māui, the fish pulled up by Māui-Pōtiki with a magic jaw-bone and cut up without permission by his brothers. Instead, the island is birthed out of the (female) Pacific Ocean. A protean, shaman-like grey wizard has impregnated the barren ocean, and watches the island grow "till the hills of it peak by peak, / Like the leaves of a flower unfolded from the soil of the untilled deep." The wizard assures the mother sea that the island is at a safe remove from "the race of pigmy men" who would despoil it. He is therefore displeased when white-skinned invaders arrive from the north and start modifying his pristine creation. The northerners, sailing under "a strange White Cross," do not understand where they are and cut down forests to build a city and sell lumber for profit. The wizard lures the children of the new arrivals into the sea and drowns them all. Their fathers attempt a rescue and a battle ensues in the breakers with the wizard who "swam as a sea-god swims." The pigmy men are torn limb from limb in the surf and their blood stains the sea. The mothers, maddened by grief, mourn their lost children and wait on the beach for word of their return from the enchanted caves of the sea; news which the narrator of the poem will divulge, having heard the whole story from the lips of a whispering sea-shell. Exchange "Wizard" for Tangaroa, god of the sea, and the story of trespass is not dissimilar from aspects of kōrero tawhito designed to establish protocols for respectful behavior towards land and kin.[24] But Tangaroa is not usually the progenitor of islands and it is made clear that the wizard's next move will be to send his creation back under the waves, in the style of Hy-Brasil and other vanishing islands. He guards the island against despoliation but there is no mention of its inhabitation by tāngata whenua ("people of the land") before the arrival of those who swarm over the beaches and flaunt a "flaring flag" over their city. As a critique of imperialist and commercial ambitions, "The Magic Island" is a fable well ahead of its time. As a pattern for retributive justice, it proposes a breathtaking symmetry between natural resources and kinship protection. The wizard revenges the harm done to his child island by killing the children of the despoilers, and leaving the doubly dispossessed mothers to wail out eternity: The mothers shall reach their kingdom when the sea hath her own again.

Mythography is one kind of map, but stories about mothers resound in Ridge's writing from its outset. The voice that calls for three small children to be cooee-ed into tea is the first cue in the drama of their disappearance in the bush ("The Three Little Children"). In the 1902 *Bulletin* version of the poem the children are toddlers, unnamed and undifferentiated; in the typescript revision they are identified as Bertie, Laurie and Fan ("The Babes of the free selector are lost on the Kendall Run!") and carefully distinguished in age so as to heighten the pathos of their imagined ordeal in the wilderness as the community tries and fails to find its lost lambs before the hawks do. In "Baby's Sick," a mother's voice summons a family member (probably her husband) home from the races in town because a young child is seriously ill, and in "The Moon Child," Monica's mother is given the last word about the disappearance of a willful daughter lured by moonlight and removed to the lunar field:

> "Whist ye," Monica's mother said,
> "Those white, quiverin', creepin' rays
> Make me think o' Monica's ways;
> Make me dream o' Monica's hair,
> Pale an' flaxen, a-shinin' there;
> An' some night when the large moon lies
> Like a flower in the fadin' skies,
> Haply Monica'll come to me—
> Lave the stars for her mother's eyes;
> Nestlin' close like she used to be,
> Warm cheek lyin' against my knee."
> —*Bulletin*, Dec. 12, 1907

It is a fairytale, and an Irish one, but the grieving mother at the cottage door watching the moon and untangling its light with a silver comb, is closely related to the mad mothers of "The Magic Island" who see the eyes and hair of their drowned children in sea pools.

Probably the most disturbing of Ridge's variations on custodial trauma is the story "A Returned Hero," published mid-1904 in the *Bulletin* and set up as a before-and-after tale of love on the sandhills under yet another moon. Max returns from the Boer war three years later to find Mona's mother at her cottage door with a grandchild and the news that her daughter took her own life out on the sandhills on Mafeking Day, after giving up hope of hearing from the lover who is now forced to take over the care of his child. He flees for Melbourne with the little girl but manages to lose her permanently and horrifically along the way. The story foreshadows Ridge's infamous poem "Lullaby" (in *The Ghetto and Other Poems*) which replays an incident from the East St. Louis race riots where a black baby was thrown alive into a burning house by a group of white women. In "The Fifth-Floor Window" from *Red Flag*[25] (published in 1927) the same unfaltering gaze informs the view of a child's body in the snow of a tenement courtyard and the open window from which her father, deserted and unemployed, says she has fallen.

Social Witness

From the fetters of Caste & Custom
—"On Zealandia"

Ridge was regarded by her early American critics as a true "poet of the people" because her immigrant background and chosen subject matter seemed readymade for the role, and because she consistently exposed the grimness of industrialized life and its human fallout. An equal and opposite impulse to ameliorative images completed her credentials as a socially engaged artist. Early signs of this consciousness are present in *Verses* and form part of its continuum with the work published in America.

Perhaps the goldfield ballads provide the clearest example in Ridge's early poems of an emergent social conscience. They are retrospective, looking back on the glory days of the West Coast of New Zealand from a present still much involved with mining and mining communities. "I was married in Hokitika Westland," she told the *Bulletin* in her 1904 note, "& saw a good deal of life on the West Coast gold diggings, where my husband was mine manager for some years." Peter Webster (1870–1946) was a shareholder in the sluicing claim of Lemain and Party established in 1891 at Kaniere

Forks, according to the Westland section of the *Cyclopedia of New Zealand*.[26] The entry includes photographs of Peter Webster and the sluicing claim, and observes that he is married to "a daughter of Mr. Daniel [sic] Macfarlane, one of the earliest settlers at Hokitika." Peter's father James Garden Webster also has a *Cyclopedia* entry noting his arrival from Scotland in 1860 and service in the Waikato Militia 1863–65, and linking him to the first miners at Kaniere in 1866. Family records show that James and Margaret Webster had thirteen children, and by the time Rosalie Ridge married their second son, his brothers and sisters were beginning to produce large families of their own around the district.[27]

The 1905 typescript has section headings "Voices of the Bush," "Songs of the Sluicers" and "Humorous Verse," and it is under the last two that the ambience of gold rush days is evoked. The ethnic diversity of the diggers and the rough justice of goldfields yarning shows up in satirical pieces like "Helblatavesky's Cow" and "The Chronicles of Sandy Gully as Kept by Skiting Bill" which fictionalize events in places already colorful in their own right. Out on the fields near Kaniere and Waimea were Liverpool Bill's, Greek's No. 1, Greek's No. 2, Italian's, Callaghan's, German Gully, Maori Gully, Red Jack's Creek, Mackay's Creek and the Scandinavian Lead. In the hastily built towns diggers could spend their money in establishments such as the Victoria Dancing Saloon (Greymouth), the Café de Paris (Hokitika) or the Casino de Venise (Charleston).[28]

"By the Mouth of the Shaft" dramatizes the recovery of a young man's body from old workings he has been prospecting alone. Here and in "A Deserted Diggings," Ridge's knowledge of mining technology and its impact on people and land alike is evident. Apart from huts like dead men's bones and a ruined forge, the scene of the deserted gully includes an overgrown truckway leading to a tunnel mouth, a rotting windlass, gravel dams and tailings, a disused gauge, flooded swamps with dead trees, axes discarded on heavily felled hillsides, rusty shovels and sluicing boxes lying as they were left when the claims "duffered out," and also:

> O'ergrown by matted bushes
>   Is the race
> Close by a ruined flume,
> Where black pipes hissed the water
>   On the "face,"
> And swart & sweating sluicers
> Drenched in the flying spume.

There would have been no shortage of derelict machinery in the area. By 1867 the combined length of Kaniere's water races totalled eighty-two miles and ground sluicing had reduced the auriferous river terraces to a fraction of their original height.[29] In a contemporary parallel with Ridge's nostalgic scene-setting, a historic walkway the length of a surviving race between the lake outlet and Kaniere Forks takes in the remains of large sections of fluming, gates, bridges and gantries from mining days. "A Deserted Diggings" ends with a predictable salute to the men whose labor and folly built "the sinews of a nation": they are "old comrades" gone before, cast in heroic mold around a rātā fire singing songs from many lands, in particular "Auld Lang Syne."

Ridge's evolving socio-political narratives also appear in "On Zealandia," where late-nineteenth century New Zealand, a "cold-eyed stranger" at the door of nationhood, is asked for a watchword by those already in the club. The reply comes back from the land itself, then from the sun shining over the "far, bright island" where community order could be different.

Ridge's proto-socialist anthem was published August 25, 1892 in *The Canterbury Times*, in the year after John Ballance's Liberal Party came to power in New Zealand, promoting the cause of Universal Suffrage among other social reforms. The poet at nineteen years old was too young to vote when women were enfranchised in 1893, but the tone and outlook of the poem foreshadow the anti-authoritarian toasts of her *Mother Earth* contributions of 1909 and 1911:

> Let men be free!
> Hate is the price
> Of servitude, paid covertly; and vice
> But the unclean recoil of tortured flesh
> Whipped through the centuries within a mesh
> Spun out of priestly art.
> Oh men, arise, be free!—Who breaks one bar
> Of tyranny in this so bitter star
> Has cleansed its bitterness in part.
> —"Freedom," *Mother Earth* 6.4, June 1911

Ridge and her mother lived on New Zealand's West Coast in the era of Richard John ("King Dick") Seddon, "the miner's friend" and larger-than-life champion of the rights of ordinary working people. Seddon became member of parliament (MP) for Hokitika in 1879 and took over from Ballance as national premier 1893–1906.[30] It was his Liberal government that passed into law the Universal Suffrage Act (1893) and the Old Age Pensions Act (1898). Seddon was also an advocate of Pacific imperialism and like most MPs of the day fiercely opposed to Chinese immigration. It is sobering to remember that radical sympathies of the late nineteenth and early twentieth centuries had deep racial biases connected with economic as well as eugenicist beliefs. Ridge's poem "The Half-Breed" was published in the *Bulletin* and is one example among many contributions to the magazine that reflect entrenched anti-Asiatic sentiment. Lola Ridge, who spoke up for the outcast and those oppressed by capitalist systems and religious orthodoxy, nevertheless shared the widespread prejudice of white, working-class Australasia against "China-men" who were perceived as a threat to jobs and the high living wage that trade unions had fought to secure. In Australia it was feared that Chinese and Melanesian (Kanaka) indentured laborers brought to work on the sugar plantations of Northern Queensland were the leading edge of an invasion that would swamp the thinly populated continent. So great were the political pressures brought to bear that the first piece of legislation passed after Federation was the Immigration Restriction Act of 1901 which put in place for half a century the policy informally known as White Australia. New Zealand had similar restrictions from 1899 and a poll tax.

Did Ridge's later experience of the American labor movement confirm or revise the anti-Chinese prejudice in her Australasian work? The depiction of Chinese in "Sun-Up" is generally neutral, even positive: Ling Ho the fruit and vegetable man sells mama loquats and a marvelous green and white cabbage. Only the nightmarish visions of the small girl's fever have "yellow faces with leering eyes / drifting in a greeny mist . . ." The detail would not rate attention except that the bogey of Ridge's story "A Returned Hero" is a clawed yellow fiend who terrorizes the two-year-old with his gibbering overtures, causing the child to leap to her death from a moving train in a wild attempt to escape his clutches. An infant's perception in a melodramatic story is backed up by adult beliefs about racial purity in "The Half-Breed," which uses a figure of infectious disease to demonize the threat of miscegenation in the backstreets of Sydney. Low black hulks glide between the Heads and moor in the gleaming bays of the city; its bustle epitomizes Ridge's vision of urban vitality ("Crowds that sever & surge & meet— / Crowds that clamour & sound along") but the schooners have landed unwelcome goods:

> Up the Strand where the white girls go,
> Down the lanes where the Half-Breeds play—

1

White & yellow, yellow & grey—
One there creeps like a shade of woe.

City, see where the Half-Breed stands:
Vain the guns at your harbour mouth!
Spawn o' the East & the hot red South
Holds your heart in her unclean hands.

Fetid foul to the sweet-breathed sea
Blows the blast from her burning lips
Floating out to the anchored ships
Drifting down on the winding Quay.

Sears the kiss of her loathsome mouth—
Spreads the blight of her poisoned veins,
Gorged & full with the blood she drains;
Ah the blood of the fresh young South!

That the terms of deformity and female horror are identical
with those used elsewhere to describe self-loathing indicates
the thoroughly conventional nature of the language of hate and
its close connections with repression and fear. In "My Care" a
psychological burden is made intimate and monstrous:

Sleep deep, my Care, in the soul of me.
Ah God! she stirs; for she knows I wis
No eyes are near us to scorn & stare
The foul misshape that her shadow is—
Crouch low in the gum tree's shade, my Care.
[. . .]
You are not meet for my friends to see:
I thrust you down with your breast all bare
To the padded cell in the soul of me;
The world is up & awake my Care.

The images of madness here, pathological and precise, are different from the more generalized romantic tumults of other poems in *Verses*. They link to a poem probably written later in Ridge's Australian years because it is not in the Mitchell Library volume, though it did appear at the end of the revised (and now lost) typescript, along with the rewritten "Parted." The address is public, as to a group of social or political conspirators:

The Insane

Near by a canary is singing,
    Whistling and singing with glee;
By the railing the prisoners are clinging—
    They, friends, who are even as we.

As we, but the world does not know it,
    The secret is ours to keep;
To guard that our eyes may not show it—
    That our lips may not babble in sleep.

For, friends, they would take us and bind us,
    Not heeding nor answering why.
In place of a world they would find us
    An acre of garden and sky.

Oh! we are the merry and glad men,
    Ye crazed, irresponsible things,
Who brand us and bind us as madmen,
    And pose as our rulers and kings.

Ye—wandering blind through the ages,
    And dazed with your schisms and schools—
Know we are the wise men and sages,
    And ye are the children and fools.

And what of the laws of your making?
        Ye say: "It is thus—it shall be";
And rise in your wrath at their breaking,
        Because ye are stronger than we.

But your rules are the ravings of fevers,
        Bred of shadows fantastic and vain,
That are spun by the little white weavers
        In the mystical loom of the brain.

They are born of your minions and creatures,
        Of the phantoms and shapes that ye saw;
But ye pose as our prophets and teachers—
        Till ye make your insanity law.

And so we are careful and cunning,
        Because ye are stronger than we,
By the railings the prisoners are sunning,
        And lo! it is sweet to be free!
        —*Bulletin*, Jan. 11, 1906

The poem is a masterpiece of inversions, moving from an
outsider's view of inmates "clinging" to the railings that sepa-
rate them from the free world to the "we" who are looking at
them "sunning" themselves on what might be the right side of
the same railings to be on. The "prisoners" have escaped from
the world of madmen and fools who would enslave them, and
whom "we" must also treat with cunning and care in order
to escape capture. "An acre of garden and sky" is not only the
boundaries of a mental institution, it is the land you will spend
a working life to freehold, effectively chained down when you
could have chosen to walk out in the world. The prisoners have
found a way to be free in their topsy-turvy world. Their exam-
ple, extreme and disturbing, reminds us that we must find a
way to do the same. The sound of Lola Ridge packing her bags

for North America and the opportunity to begin over again is unmistakable.

The Transnationals

> *Throwing an ephemeral glory about life's vanishing points*
> —"Manhattan," *The Ghetto and Other Poems*

It is Wednesday, November 11, 1903. On Sydney Harbor the *Mokoia*, inbound from Wellington, is approaching the Union Steam Ship wharves at Margaret and Sussex streets after a four-day crossing in unsettled conditions. For two of her passengers, mother and daughter, the moment reprises an earlier arrival, when one brought the other from Dublin to Sydney as a child. Waiting for them then were aunt, uncle and cousins for the little girl; sister, brother-in-law and nephews for the mother. Waiting for them now are widowed aunt and grown-up cousins with children older and younger than the three-year-old boy who travels with the two women. "I am an Australian by sympathy & association," his mother will write to the *Bulletin* editor a few months later, invoking the years between three and perhaps six that remain so clear in her memory; watching her son begin a transplanted life of his own. They will not stay in Sydney but it is the place more than any other that has allowed passage between worlds, an *entrepôt* she is glad to be stepping into again.

The Shipping Masters Office begins its tally of those disembarking the *Mokoia*, saloon class first. *Mesd. Quirk Govett McFarlane* writes the clerk. And four lines later in the same boxed column: *Mesdames Watson Master Webster*, adding & *infant* below the last name.[31] The women and the child come ashore into the early summer heat and are lost to view. Years later, in *Sun-Up and Other Poems*, the collection that houses her double-lensed poem of antipodean childhood (for Keith Webster ghosts Rose Ridge as surely as Jude shadows Betty), Lola Ridge names the city where memory, ever parenthetical, moves in overlapping circles:

The Dream

I have a dream
to fill the golden sheath
of a remembered day. . . .
(Air
heavy and massed and blue
as the vapor of opium. . .
domes
fired in sulphurous mist. . .
sea
quiescent as a gray seal. . .
and the emerging sun
spurting up gold
over Sydney, smoke-pale, rising out of the bay. . . .)
But the day is an up-turned cup
and its sun a junk of red iron
guttering in sluggish-green water—
where shall I pour my dream?

Questions remain. What is the extent of Lola Ridge's Australasian production? Are there more publications in unindexed periodicals and newspapers? Are there more paintings and drawings in New Zealand and from the four years of art-making in Sydney? What was Ridge reading in these years and who was she writing or talking to apart from A. G. Stephens? These and other questions will be answered by ongoing biographical and bibliographical research, and by the appearance of a *Collected Poems* that takes account of the formative years spent in Australia and New Zealand.

Meanwhile it is clear that Ridge elided her New Zealand life after leaving the country and her marriage, and that she had reason to further conceal herself and her son as they moved towards North America in 1907. Perhaps it was also necessary to conceal the poems that pointed to New Zealand. Ridge claimed that she destroyed a poetry manuscript after leaving Sydney,[32] but if she did so, it did not prevent her from contributing poems from *Verses* to the *Overland Monthly*, *Gunter's Magazine* and *Ainslee's* 1908–11 (ten poems) and 1920 (one poem).

Lola Ridge is a transnational figure whose full outline we are now beginning to see. In America she has been grouped with women artists of the Left and with literary Modernists, but how interesting it would be to compare her work and career with, for example, that of Emma Goldman (1869–1933) and Gertrude Stein (1874–1945), each of whom moved from first worlds (Russia, the United States) that continued to inflect their experience of a second world (the United States, France). In Australia, Ridge's work needs to be compared with that of other *Bulletin* contributors: Henry Lawson, Banjo Paterson and Adam Lindsay Gordon are near contemporaries; Will H. Ogilvie, E. J. Brady, Arthur H. Adams, Roderick Quinn, Victor Daley, Hubert Church and Bernard O'Dowd all published first collections under Stephens' *Bulletin* imprint. But perhaps there are women artists and writers of the period who mirror Ridge's remarkable bolt for personal and artistic freedom: Louise Mack (1870–1935), the only woman to have a volume of poetry published by Stephens, offers some parallels, as does Miles Franklin (1879–1954).

In New Zealand it is possible to make out some generational connections that emphasize the importance of transnational identity: Frances Hodgkins (1869–1947), Blanche Baughan (1870–1958), G. B. Lancaster (1873–1945) and Jane Mander (1877–1949) all performed variations on the need to escape home ground and social conventions in order to write or paint. But the most resonant comparison to another woman artist lies elsewhere. A lifetime of movement between countries and aesthetic breakthrough into a congenial Modernism followed by a return to traditional metrical forms are characteristics also of Ursula Bethell (1874–1945), whose first book *From a Garden in the Antipodes* (1929) is considered one of the touchstones of modern New Zealand poetry. Ridge's means were different but the achievement of *The Ghetto and Other Poems* and *Sun-Up and Other Poems* holds a similar position in American traditions of the literary Left. In Bethell's archive too is evidence of the pre-Garden poet, writing and painting in the 1890s and early 1900s but much taken up by social work and spiritual directing until the apparent serendipity of the free verse poems enclosed with letters to friends in England set in train her first book publication. The major difference between Bethell and Ridge is one of background and education, but it would be instructive to map Bethell's genteel North Canterbury upbringing against Ridge's altogether rougher years on the West Coast, and to count not one but two incipient Modernists transiting an adoptive country.

Ridge's voice drifts back from New York in *The Ghetto and Other Poems*, addressing a company that extends across one continent and looks back even as it projects a future that is liminal, lucent and inclusive:

To the Others

I see you, refulgent ones,
Burning so steadily
Like big white arc lights. . .
There are so many of you.
I like to watch you weaving—
Altogether and with precision
Each his ray—

Your tracery of light,
Making a shining way about America.

I note your infinite reactions—
In glassware
And sequin
And puddles
And bits of jet—
And here and there a diamond...

But you do not yet see me,
Who am a torch blown along the wind,
Flickering to a spark
But never out.

Notes

1. Lola Ridge, *Verses*. Unpublished carbon typescript [1905]. 93 pp. Papers of Alfred George Stephens, 1859–1933. MLMSS 4937/10. Mitchell Library, State Library of New South Wales.

2. Daniel Tobin, "Modernism, Leftism, and the Spirit: The Poetry of Lola Ridge," in Lola Ridge, *Selected Early Poems of Lola Ridge*, ed. D. Tobin (2007: vii–xli).

3. Ridge's literary executor Elaine Sproat is preparing a full-length biography and a collected edition of her work. For this introduction I have drawn on bio-bibliographical material by Stanley J. Kunitz (*Living Authors: A Book of Biographies*, ed. Dilly Tante. 1931: 340–41), Allen Guttmann (*Notable American Women 1607–1950*, ed. James *et al.*, Vol. 3. 1971: 158–60), Peter Quartermain (*American Poets 1880–1945*, ed. Quartermain. 1993: 355–61), William Drake (*The First Wave: Women Poets in America, 1915–1945*. 1987), Nancy Berke (*American Women Writers 1900–1945*, ed. Champion. 2000: 295–301 and *Women Poets on the Left: Lola Ridge, Genevieve Taggard, Margaret Walker*. 2001). To these materials I have added documentary record from Australasian sources presented in Michele Leggott, "The First Life: A Chronology of Lola Ridge's Australasian Years" (BLUFF 06, NZ Electronic

Poetry Centre [nzepc], 2006) and "Lola Ridge Journal Publication 1892–1920" (*Ka Mate Ka Ora* 12, 2013: 119–28). See also Lola Ridge Author Page, NZ Electronic Poetry Centre (2018) for full-text reproduction of Ridge's New Zealand and Australian journal publications. Thanks to Elaine Sproat for reading and responding to drafts of the essay on which this introduction is based. Thanks to Terese Svoboda, whose *Anything That Burns You: A Portrait of Lola Ridge, Radical Poet* (2016) has filled in more of Ridge's extraordinary life. Thanks also to Peter Quartermain who first alerted me to Ridge's antipodean background.

4. Theresia Liemlienio Marshall, "New Zealand Literature in the Sydney Bulletin 1880–1930" (Ph.D. thesis, University of Auckland, 1995) lists Ridge's *Bulletin* contributions 1901–07. The Australian Literature database adds publication from *The Australian Town and Country Journal* and *The Lone Hand*. Line drawings by Ridge accompany her short story "The Trial of Ruth," *New Zealand Illustrated Magazine* (Aug. 1903): 343–48. Elaine Sproat, in an email communication with Michele Leggott on Aug. 12, 2012, notes that she has found eight drawings from the Australasian period (including a self-portrait) and five later works.

5. David Lawson, Interview, Brooklyn, Nov. 17, 1977. In Paul Avrich, *Anarchist Voices: An Oral History of Anarchism in America* (1995: 198–99).

6. Research by Elaine Sproat brought to light Keith Webster's subsequent history, and contact with his daughters Gloria and Gladys Bernand-Wehner of Santiago, Chile, was made in early 2011.

7. Lola Ridge, *The Ghetto and Other Poems* (New York: B. W. Huebsch, 1918).

8. Lola Ridge, *Sun-Up and Other Poems* (New York: B. W. Huebsch, 1920).

9. Concerning the H. M. Greville Company, see Alun Eirug Davies, "Paper-Mills and Paper-Makers in Wales 1700–1900," *National Library of Wales Journal* (Summer 1967). The seven transcribed watermarks of the Mitchell typescript appear as variations on a paper styled "Super Royal 42th" (or "52th" or "Imperial 78th").

10. George Mackaness and Walter W. Stone, eds., *The Books of The Bulletin 1880–1952* (1955).

11. Papers of Alfred George Stephens, 1859–1933. MLMSS 4937/29. Mitchell Library, State Library of New South Wales.

12. Ibid., MLMSS 4937/28.

13. In an email communication on Aug. 12, 2012, Elaine Sproat noted that she located the revised typescript of "Verses by Lola Ridge" and received photocopies of some pages from Kathleen Brooks, the daughter of Ridge's cousin John Edmund Miles Penfold. The revised typescript was sixty-one pages. All but two of the poems ("Forgive dear heart. . ." and "Song of the Earth") were carried over from the first typescript. The collection ended with "The Moon Child," "The Scented Garden," "The Insane" and "Parted." Except for the pages held by Sproat, this revised typescript has since been lost.

14. "Waiting" is itemized in the contents pages of the Mitchell Library Verses (as manuscript pages 56–57) but the entry has been crossed out and these two pages are missing from the typescript. The poem was present in the revised typescript (see Note #13 above).

15. L. Clunie, "Katipō spider. What is this bug? A guide to common invertebrates of New Zealand." Manāki Whenua Landcare Research, 2004.

16. Phillip Ross May, *The West Coast Gold Rushes*. 2nd ed. (1967: 194).

17. Lola Ridge, "The Bush," *The Lone Hand*, Dec. 1, 1908: 176-77.

18. Ursula Bethell, *Collected Poems*, 2nd ed. Ed. O'Sullivan (1997: 34).

19. Lola Ridge, Autobiography for *Sydney Bulletin*, Jan. 27, 1904. 3 pp. Papers of Alfred George Stephens, 1859–1933. MLMSS 4937/28. Mitchell Library, State Library of New South Wales.

20. Drake, 187–89.

21. Ibid., 188.

22. Casebook. Hokitika Lunatic Asylum / Mental Hospital (Seaview). R18946512. 1888–1906. Archives New Zealand.

23. Elsdon Best, "Comets," *The Astronomical Knowledge of the Maori* (1922: 54–57).

24. For a summary of kōrero tawhito, see "Te Ao Māori Tawhito" *He Hīnātore Ki Te Ao Māori / A Glimpse of the Māori World: Māori Perspectives on Justice. Part 1: Traditional Māori Concepts*. New Zealand Ministry of Justice, 2001.

25. Lola Ridge, *Red Flag* (New York: Viking, 1927).

26. *Cyclopedia of New Zealand*, Vol. 5: Nelson, Marlborough and Westland Provincial Districts (Cyclopedia Company, 1906).

27. Alison Clarke, "The Webster Family." Unpublished notes supplied to Michele Leggott, 2006.

28. May, 194, 310.

29. Ibid., 227.

30. R. M. Burdon. "Seddon, Richard John (1845–1906)." *Encyclopedia of New Zealand*, ed. McLintock (Reed, 1966).

31. "Mokoia. 11 November 1903." *State Records of New South Wales. Shipping Master's Office: Passenger Arrivals*; ref X286, microfilm number 2015.

32. Guttmann, 158.

VOICES OF THE BUSH

/

Under Song

The mystical, the strong
        Deep-throated Bush,
Is humming in the hush
        Low bars of song:
Far singing in the trees
        In tongues unknown—
A reminiscent tone
        On minor keys:

Boughs swaying to & froe,
        Though no winds pass—
Strange odours in the grass
        Where no flow'rs grow;
Faint fluttering of wings,
        And birds' sweet vows
Once babbled on the boughs
        Of faded springs.

The murmur in the air
        That ebbs & waves,
Is music from the graves
        Of all things fair;
And mingles in the still
        Of twilight's hush,
With voices of the Bush
        From swamp & hill.

One seeking through the husk
　　Of darkness thrown,
May hear it through lone,
　　Grave halls of dusk,
Low ringing in his ears;
　　And ponder long
The meaning of the song
　　He faintly hears.

At Sun-Down

The Bush is leaning like a tired child,
Her dear head nestling on the breast of night,
Fast glooming now above the pine girt height;
The strife of cities & their tumult wild—
I seem to hear it as a far-off fight.

Beneath the flutter of the rising stars,
Beyond the ratas where the red sun dips
Are bays & galaxies of fair white ships;
A dull surf booms upon the distant bars—
The cities call me with a million lips!

The Bush bends o'er me with her wond'rous, long
Wind-loosened hairs on my unquiet breast,
Whose barred thoughts burning to confront the test,
With glowing impulse & endeavour strong
To rise & answer when they call the rest!

The night is coming, & the shadows trail
Like wasted lives across the forest belt;
The red clouds battle on a crimson veldt,
Like storied heroes—how they charge & fail!
And strange forms mingle as they fade & melt.

Ah God: the strife for a remembered name!
I hear the turbulent, dull roar, the din
Of that wide vortex drawing all things in
About its circle to the crest of fame,
Some rise to forfeit & some stoop to win.

The upward shadow of the broad earth meets
The sky-line, golden as a young life's rim,
All dark beneath but bubbles at the brim:
My heart is throbbing for the roar of streets—
The cloister of the Bush is screened & dim.

Dawn on the Mountains

'Tis the coming of the Dawn,
With her golden head unveiling—
How the clinging shadows fawn
On the robes about her trailing,
    Where dark gullies yawn.

With the stars about her girth,
Night the Wanton, low is kneeling,
Hiding from the mocking mirth—
Hiding from the laughter stealing
    O'er the face of earth.

And the ranges far-away
Slow their massive heads are lifting
From their couches soft & grey,
All the vapour curtains rifting,
    Letting in the day.

Where the dead moon drifts on high
And the ways of light are glowing,
Clouds transparent floating by,
Crimson dawning glories growing—
    Ratas of the sky!

O'er the gleaming peaks they go,
Golden shadows interwoven;
And their shining largesse throw
Where the mountain mist is cloven—
      Flushing the white snow.

In a choir of leafage dim
Waking birds sing on the ledges,
Greeting with a pagan hymn
The sun-king on the edges
      Of the forest rim.

Light & laughter in the air,
As each roving sunbeam pushes
Prying fingers everywhere;
Eyes obliquely through the bushes
      Darting here & there.

Down the day-coast one is borne—
Dawn with golden eyes fast closèd,
And the sun-webs round her drawn—
Dawn with fair white limbs composèd
      On the bier of morn.

Lake Kanieri

Blue veined & dimpling, dappled in the sun
Lies Lake Kanieri, like a tired child
Wide-eyed, close clinging to the spacious skirts
Of old Tuhua, the big brawny nurse
On whose broad lap I lie. All else is still.
A bird's near whistle is the only sound
That in the silence beats into my brain
Insistent, shrill. Now is no need to serve
Or suffer or regret: it seems life holds
No future & no past for me but this
Sun-lighted mountain & the brooding bush.

Nor art nor history nor written page
Could touch me now; it is enough to be
And feel the slow & rhythmic pulse of earth
Beat under me; & see the low red sun
Stoop o'er the massive shoulders of the range.
Oh, lone, heroic, melancholy Hills!
Your dim, gaunt peaks stand in the afterglow
Like Duty, stern, implacable & cold;
Remote from the harsh clamour of the plains,
And murmur of men's cities all unheard.
Oh, still & calm; Oh, pure & wise & strong!
My restless heart from your locked hearts shut out,
Leans on your strength & craves the peace you hold—
Peace born of conflict. Ye old Stoic Hills!
Yield up your secrets. On your furrowed fronts

Are scars of fierce upheavals; in your grave,
Deep breasts what dreams are shut? Ye seem to stand
Like pale, impassive monks, whose chill looks hide
Forbidden memories of clinging lips,
Of passion conquered & of pain repressed
Within their breasts congealed. With outlines dim
The hooded slopes, like meek nuns grouped in prayer,
Kneel in the screened cloister of the bush
Dark robed & secret; & the laughing lake,
Smoothed by the slow, cool fingers of the Dusk,
Has coiled herself to sleep. The light is gone,
Save on those heights where Day, grown weak & old,
Close by the dying embers of the sun
Sits like an old man musing on his past.

The Bush

The gay winds fondle with the maiden Bush,
Who sways & quivers in their close embrace;
And from her broad brow all the stray locks push,
That fall in tresses o'er her elfin face.

The rival sunbeams their bold fingers thrust
Amid her guarded & most secret sweets;
They steal & nestle on her swelling bust,
And view unchidden all her chaste retreats.

And when the Day upon his molten track
Draws them in meshes to his gleaming woof,
Each, wistful, glances like a lover back,
Where still, inscrutable, she sits aloof.

I lie a-dreaming in the twilight hush
Beside a pool wherein the first star glows,
With mute hands reaching to the great, grey Bush,
Who all things seeing; understands & knows.

Her grim trees standing in impassive lines—
Know they of secrets that can find no tongue?
The crumbling timbers of these fallen pines
Were straight green saplings when the world was young.

Oh men! heart-tired of unquiet days,
Of sad lives sundered, & strong purpose bent
By Life's denial of thy meed of praise;
Come share the largesse of her clean content.

And weary women who have seen love droop
In lust & laughter, till thy bruised hearts yearn,
Some help that stooping shall not seem to stoop,
Seek peace & counsel in her ways of fern.

And ye, her nursling, who would turn the key
Her shut heart closes on its hidden things,
Go learn & listen at her mother knee
The half-articulate, deep song she sings.

Dead-Pine Shadows

The dead-pines stood like pickets
Beside the long, white road,
High o'er the terrace faces
Their sin'ster shadows strode;
And through the tangled thickets
The woven moon-shine sprayed
The road with lightsome places,
But more was in the shade.

The dead-tree shadows muster
Life's long white road beside,
And forth in stealthy batches
Of gaunt, grey shapes they ride;
But high the joy-beams cluster,
And through Life's twisted glade
They fall in gleaming patches
On barren leagues of shade.

The Hour of Dawn

The great, slow brain of the earth is waking;
      O'er the solar skies
The white Dawn comes & the light is breaking
      From her half-shut eyes.

As slow she moves with her long skirts trailing
      O'er the forest rims,
She lifts her robe of the grey nun's veiling
      From her gleaming limbs.

To praise of birds she has stayed to listen
      Where the locked boughs meet;
Her cold cheek warms & the dewdrops glisten
      On her bare white feet.

All sounds are still, & the soul is shaken
      As it stands alone:
The best & worst in the heart must waken
      That the heart hath known.

And darkness falls by the day supplanted;
      With her eyes alight
The Morning stands with her fair feet planted
      On the prostrate Night.

The strong hearts leap & the weak ones sicken
    At the sound of strife
Of thoughts that leap & the deeds that quicken
    In the womb of Life.

On the Track

I grope in my soul's dim places—
The cells that are screened in black,
And peer till I find the faces
Of two on a sunlit track—
Oh! grey were the great bush spaces,
That flung us our wild words back.

I laughed when I heard you sigh it—
"Good-by," but no word I said,
The blood in my veins ran riot;
I stayed not your parting tread.
How cool was the dusk & quiet,
And line of the far sky red.

At night I steal from the sleepers,
To watch where the breakers reach
And strike at the white surf reapers,
Their scythes to the shaven beach;
Like thoughts that have slain their keepers,
And mock at the creed they preach.

Day comes with its jar & wrangle—
I fret at the sunbeam's glare;
For what is their tinsel spangle
To shimmering gold they were!
A-shine on the twisted tangle
Of cones in my unbound hair.

I yield to a dream entreating—
A path that is known to two,
With shadowy branches meeting,
And sunshine filtering through—
But never a glance of greeting,
Or word as I pass by you!

In the Shadow

I forgot the voices calling—
Calling to me through the air,
For the warm clasp of your fingers,
And your lips upon my hair;

I forgot the pride of lineage,
I forsook the hope of fame—
I'd ha' left the road to heaven
For the magic of your name.

If you loved but as the many,
And my soul you never knew;
All my very life & being
Was but one long thought of you.

Now your eyes are cold & callous
And your lips are turned away,
And the brightest light from heaven
Is a shadow on my day.

All the mighty bush is gleaming
In the glitter of the sun;
But my thoughts are folded round me,
Like the dark robes of a nun.

Think of Me Not With Sadness

Think not of me with sad thoughts
Decked out in mourning grey,
But weave a woof about me
Of colours gold & gay;
For if I were your own, love,
We might regret—some day.

Streams at their source united
Have yet diverging flowed;
Be mine the twisted pathway,
And yours the trampled road;
Who choose uncharted ways, love,
Find few to share their load.

With thought of me, say never:
"Her love was false & vain
As sun-cloud of the dawning
That falls at noon in rain!"
Let not the thought of me, love,
Be one to bring you pain.

Think when you roam the forest,
And o'er its ways you see
The sunshine on the Kauries
And flash of bird & bee,
Mid all things pure & bright, love,
Some fond, light thought of me.

To an Old Playfellow

I remember the far green hill-top,
Where we clung to the rata vines,
And you climbed to the nesting parrots
In the boughs of the Kaurie pines:

And the scent of the tutu bushes
By the bend in the path o'ergrown,
Where you wove me a necklet of rushes,
As we sat on the "Bunyip stone."

I remember the long bright mornings
When we waded the shallow creeks,
Where the quartz & the mica glittered
In the pools of the stony deeps;

And the day that we roamed the terrace
Mid the tangle of supple vines;
And the tuis sang on the meros
To the locusts' hum in the pines.

But the wind came out of the forest
Like a lost soul's moan in the air,
Till we thought 'twas the great Bush Spirit,
Who would draw us & hold us there;

And the might of our child-hearts failed us
As we fled from the forest door,
With the roar of the pines behind us,
And the known, green flats before.

Shriveled now are the tutu bushes,
That we climbed with our light limbs then;
And the shrine of the hill-side echoes
To the clang of the tools of men:

But the mystical pines lean over,
And their shadows are falling black
Between one on the trampled high-way,
And a chum on an old bush track.

The Summons

The Voice of the North Wind is calling;
And night answers heavy & slow,
Her brows glooming sullen & low;
Their loose stirrups clashing & falling
The foam horses buffet & blow.

The bush loometh darkly before us,—
A dim & indefinite form,
Where lightning leaps vivid & warm,
And mad winds are shouting in chorus
The muster "to arms!" of the storm.

Importunate, loud & persistent,
The Storm Spirits call to my own—
A prayer or command in their tone
That reaches me rousing, insistent,
Me—helpless & sick & alone!

Do ye weary of leaping & falling?
Oh, North Winds so merry & mad?
Why mock ye the dreams I once had?
Exhorting, & rousing & calling
Me—lonely & sullen & sad!

The Three Little Children

Just three little children playing, all brown with the wind & sun;
Wee Bertie, the baby toddling, but Laurie & Fan could run
In chase of the glancing beetles, the bright & elusive things,
That shook as they whirled above them the dust from their golden wings.

The 'possum came out of the gum tree in midst of their laughing play,
And fled from the little children who followed & lost their way,
Up over the grass-sown paddocks & far from the home in view,
Deep into the grim bush shadows & out of the world they knew.

How late were the children playing! "Loo, cooee them in to tea—
They're down by the scented wattles, or up in the grey gum tree."
But vain was our eager calling, till slow o'er the looming plain
The night like a witch was crouching, encloaked in a drifting rain:
"All hands of the shearing stations, come out with the rising sun
The Babes of the free selector are lost on the Kendall Run!"
But blurred were the slender traces; for night was enleagued with Hell,
And safe was the bush & secret—she guarded her counsel well.

God! why did the rain fall faster—why kept not the wind at bay
For sake of the little children who wandered & lost their way?
And why did the morning sun beat like flame on the steaming sands,
To burn on the rain-wet faces & blister the small, weak hands?
We watched as the third dawn lifted the lids of her slow grey eyes
The shape of a vulture sailing far out o'er a distant rise;
A blot on the clean blue sky-line, a-wheel on a circling track;
As loudly we called the children the scream of the hawk came back.

"'Tis only a death-bird gloating—some lamb lost out on the plain,"
But rousing the sleeping trackers, we took up the quest again.
We came upon a white sun-bonnet caught fast on a bramble hedge,
A space in the broken bushes, & there on the stony ledge
Young Bertie, the babe, was lying locked close in the arms of Fan—
The woman is aye the mother—& Laurie, the wee, brave man,
A stick in his wasted fingers, & face to the cruel crows. . . .
Afar o'er the pale horizon the glittering sun arose,
And threw on the small still faces the light of the great, white day,
But the souls of the little children had long ago lost their way.

The Incurable

The slow lagging day is now over,
And cut like the blade of a sword,
A red bar of sunshine is hanging
Athwart the white wall of the ward.

I lean by the window with Alice
Linked, watching the grey shadows push
Gaunt arms reaching east to the Dead-house,
And south to the roll of the bush:

"'Twas years ago—three last September—
They carried me here in the spring;
They said I should go ere the summer—"
She touches the band of my ring;

"I'll never wear one on my finger—
Not that it will matter for much!"
Her bright head turned out to the sun-down
Leans low on the arm of her crutch.

I talk of old days on the ranges,
And show her the snow-saddled peak
We climbed on a long faded summer,
Till brightness comes back to her cheek,

That dimples with easy forgetting
Of light natures deepened by pain;
And slowly the lumbering shadows
Crawl over the bush broken plain.

They'll carry her east to the Dead-house
In hush of some rain-ridden morn—
For some is it life to be buried?
For some is it death to be born?

The sunset is red on her tresses
That glitter like bubbles on wine,
Wind-shaken, they blow from the window
Against the dull sable of mine.

And even out there in the Dead-house—
As light draweth light to its fold—
I know a stray sunbeam would find them,
And nestle there—gold to the gold!

When the Moon Was in Eclipse

It was night upon the grey-downs,
And the moon was near eclipse,
  As they lay beside the sheep;
One a-babbling in his dreaming
Of white arms & clinging lips,
  Moved & murmured in his sleep.

And the other crouched & listened
To the wild swans in their flight,
  And the tinkling of the team:
As a shadow leaned across him
That was blacker than the night—
  Did it break the sleeper's dream?

"Waken, Una, raise the window—
Let me climb into your nest;"
  Thus he muttered as he slept,
"Nestle closer, dear one, closer!
Till you lie upon my breast,"
  And the shadow nearer crept;

"What of bonds & creeds & symbols?
All the name words & the dross—
  They are not for us Mine Own!
High above the lonely grey-downs,
Sits our priest the great white Cross;
  And athwart your window thrown,

"The moon-shine & shadow mingles,
Even as your soul & mine;
            And the pale curve of your cheek,
Like a fair & folded flower
Drooping, as your warm limbs twine,
            And your arms about me creep.

"Love can know no law but loving—
Let them curse with Book & Bell!
            As I swoon upon your lips,
In the circle of my heaven,
While their lying murmurs tell—"
            And the moon was in eclipse.

One was strong with strength of hatred,
One with mazed & maddened brain:
            The low moon hung shadow spanned,
And the night was dark as passion,
And the wind was cold as pain,
            As it moaned above the sand.

Bob, the collie, leaped & listened:
If the silly things would rove,
            Then good-by to peaceful sleep!
And he panted through the darkness
As he trotted round the drove—
            It was nothing with the sheep.

*   *   *   *   *

As the moon & shadow parted,
Dawn, the stealthy tracker came
        Gained upon him as he crept;
Till he leaned above her bedside,
Calling harshly on her name—
        Strange—how heavily she slept!

Freshly through the open lattice
The keen, early wind blew in,
        And a blurred & blotted sheet—
The last witness of her falsehood,
And the seal upon her sin,
        Fluttered lightly to his feet:

"Can you hear me, my beloved?
Where the sloping headland dips
        To brown tussock & grey mounds,
Faint & far the swans are calling,
And the moon is near eclipse
        High above the looming downs.

"And my heart is strange to-night, dear,
How it flutters & is still!
        But it may be better soon;
And a subtle, deadly menace
Seems to hold me like a chill—
        'Tis the eclipse of the moon!"

Never more for clasp of passion,
Never more for man's desire!
     Slow he lifted up her hand,
And a ray blue as her eyeflash,
Glittered from a pale sapphire
     On her finger jewel-spanned.

It was day upon the grey-downs,
And the early sunshine fell,
     As he muttered with white lips:
"You have met your lover, Una;
For you followed him to hell
     When the moon was in eclipse!"

Moon-Struck

"She is yellow & blond & bare
With a flame in her eye-balls lit,
As she floats where the star-men sit—
Pale mask with a light behind;
And she gloats as she holds me there
In the strands of her twisted hair,
Me—dazzled & dazed & blind!

"With a grin on her faded face,
Like a bawd of the skies she leers,
And gibbers & jibes & jeers
At me as I writhe in vain,
Till I tear at the flimsy lace,
With the web of a goblin trace,
She tangles about my brain.

"See her locks on the wind a-swirl,
And the flash of a gleaming limb,
As she lolls on the mountain rim
Her cheek to the leaning sky:
And the star-men around her whirl
For a touch of the white-faced girl
Who drifts like a vapour by.

"But I know that her foils are set—
I can see by the grin she wears
She has baited her golden snares:
'Deep deep of my opal bowl,
Ye shall drink, & forget—forget!'
But I strain at the strong white net
Whose coils are about my soul!"

It was night by the op'ning stars,
As he lay with his face upturned
Where the eyes of her blazed & burned:
Now she passeth exulting, slow—
It is dawn by the closing stars—
With a soul in her strong, white bars,
And a mindless hulk below.

My Care

I laugh good-night as their foot-falls die—
A flung-back jest & a repartee:
The star-buds blow in the twilight sky:
Sleep deep, my Care, in the soul of me.
Ah God! she stirs; for she knows I wis
No eyes are near us to scorn & stare
The foul misshape that her shadow is—
Crouch low in the gum tree's shade, my Care.

Neath wind-bent boughs where the moon-shine slips
And sets her brow with a single pearl,
And sprays her cheeks & her burning lips,
She leans forlorn as a pleading girl.
Her eyes are wet with a hopeless prayer—
My eyes are callous & hard & dry—
A late bird speeds through the stagnate air,
And circles wide as it passes by.

*　*　*　*　*

The moon hath set in a golden ring,
The blind stars beg at the gates of day;
And you—that grope at my heart & cling
With face distorted & drawn & grey—
You are not meet for my friends to see:
I thrust you down with your breast all bare
To the padded cell in the soul of me;
The world is up & awake my Care.

Song of the Earth

When the light o' the far heaven changes
      Through the day's broken bars,
O'er the peaks of the mystical ranges
      I arise with the stars;

But I pass in a wreath o' white vapour,
      When the shadows are done,
And the arms of the sloping hills taper
      To the reach of the sun.

All the wild winds are huddled together,
      Lying low in their lair,
Falls the down of a lone eagle's feather
      Like a stone in the air.

Oh Beloved! my bosom is dreary
      As the lilt of a song,
When the heart of the singer is weary,
      And the rhythm is long.

For I hear not thy voice as I listen
      Lying here on the turf,
As I watch for thy white limbs to glisten
      On the crest of the surf.

Is there aught 'neath the wide sky's embowment
        Like thy mighty unrest?
Oh, to lie for one lingering moment
        On thy turbulent breast!

How I long for thy waters to hold me,
        As they lap at my feet,
To flow over & fondle & fold me
        Till our joy were complete.

To inundate me, saturate, press me,
        Over mountain & fen,—
Oh, arise in your strength & possess me
        From the cities of men!

"Forgive dear heart. . ."

Forgive dear heart, dear love, Forgive!
That I so lean upon your strength
For in your soul my soul would live
And leaps & strains its bridle length

Through all the busy noon I fend
A dream of you that sits apart
But when the hours their labours end
It knocks & enters in my heart.

And there the long still night; it lies,
So closed & warm upon my breast,
As bird that flies to alien skies
At even flutters to its nest.

The Parting

I held my pleading arms to you—
Pale lips that faltered to confess,
Of all the store of joys we knew
To cull one bittersweet caress.

Your eyes were stern & cold & still;
Their bleak looks frosted o'er my heart,
Ere I could lean upon my will
You thrust my clinging hands apart.

Oh, love, good-by when waters run
To peaks that glitter far & high;
When meek earth fronts the frowning sun,
And stays her circle in the sky.

When 'possums mount on moon-shine bars,
And glow-worms hidden in the mine,
Shall leave their caves to mock the stars—
Oh, then my lips shall meet with thine!

On Zealandia

"Ye who stand as a cold-eyed stranger,
Give your watchword," the nations cry,
And a wind from the rolling forest
Whispers low as it wanders by:
        "On Zealandia"

It is murmured along the ranges
It is sung where the great pines grow
It is heard on the wild grey beaches
Where the pipes of the white surf blow
        On Zealandia

Ask the sun of the wide skies' rover,
As he stares through his molten bars,
If he shines on a land that's fairer
In the range of a thousand stars
        Than Zealandia?

Let him gather his roaming children,
Let him ask of his rambling beams—
They may know of a far, bright island
In the flight of their starward dreams
        Like Zealandia?

Up, oh Child of the great Pacific!
And arise from your morning sleep;
Though the feet of a nation stumble,
Let the heart of a nation leap—
　　　On Zealandia!

Ye are one of the fearless vanguard,
Where the free Battalion leads
Ye shall stoke at the blazing furnace,
Where the fuel is thoughts & deeds—
　　　On Zealandia

When the thrones of the world are fallen,
And your word shall be weighed & known,
As the voice of a mighty people,
Of the tribes to a nation grown—
　　　Young Zealandia.

From the fetters of Caste & Custom
And their faiths & their symbols free;
From the bonds of their old traditions,
That are sunk in your circling sea—
　　　On Zealandia!

Sleep Dolores

"Sleep Dolores," my mother sang to me
When Life was like a rose, dear,
Just opening round & red;
Quaint, fantastic, wayward melody—
Now life is dreary prose, dear,
And all its songs are said!

"Sleep Dolores; the grey wolves ride away,"
I saw them in a far line
Across the looming plains—
"Sleep Dolores! Sweet slumber while you may,—"
(Gaunt shapes athwart the star-line,
That broke their bridle reins.)

"Sleep Dolores!" In that old world o' mine
Where fancy vainly lingers,
Were palaces to let;
No gates, toll gates, nor title deeds to sign,
Nor tangle of cold fingers
That never should have met!

"Sleep Dolores." I thought the shining stars
Were lamps along the Night-Coast
Of cities far away;
Head lights, red lights that flashed among the spars
Of schooners on the White-Coast
A-down the Milky Way.

"Sleep Dolores," & tranced in slumber song
Bright wond'rous things I saw dear
My starry cities in
Child dreams, wild dreams that recked not right or wrong?
And Love was over Law, dear,
And knew not sex or sin.

"Hush Dolores, the wolves are near the town!"
A thrust, a thin red knife line—
The blade is sharp & keen:
"Wake Dolores! the grey wolves ride thee down—
Gaunt shapes athwart thy life-line,
And not a league between!"

The Legend of the Cross

A star—the brightest shining
Of all his gleaming race—
Once for the dark Earth pining,
Sighed o'er lone leagues of space;
But scarce she heard him suing—
So faint & far his ray:
Till in his eager wooing
He left the Milky Way.

He heard the moon call to him,
But paused not in his flight;
The planets hardly knew him
Swift shooting through the night.
He passed the Sisters Seven,
Bright-eyed & cold & high;
To all the stars in heaven
He whispered a good-by.

The Earth, a dusky maiden,
Stirred in her vestal dreams,
Her deep eyes slumber laden,
Dazed in his burning beams;
Close in his arms he wound her,
And with her tangled hair,
The forests braided round her,
She screened her bosom bare.

Her breasts, two mountains swelling,
Rose soft & round & white,
Her heart's loud clamour quelling
She clasped the son of Light;
Bathed in his glist'ning splendour,
His star-eyes on her face,
In trembling sweet surrender
She sank in his embrace.

But, ah, sad words to ponder—
How apt is love to sate!
Those boundless spaces yonder,
His aerial estate—
The welkin scarce could span it—
So faint & vast & far:
Was Earth—dull, lowly planet!
Fit mate for crested star?

He sped, ere Earth had missed him,
'Neath cover of the day
Fast through the Solar System,
Past where the Milky Way
Hung o'er the roof of heaven
Like nebula of pearls,
Back to the Sisters Seven,
That group of high-born girls.

Dull wak'ning of the "after"
That she who loves must learn!
Earth heard the fairies' laughter,
As 'mid the screening fern
They lurked, await for plunder,
Where dazed by glare o' day,
Weak eyes a-light with wonder—
The starry children lay.

But Dusk, the secret guessing
Drew near to hide their birth,
With cool, kind hands caressing
The fevered brow of Earth;
Where first the prying day leaves
The long dim forest busk,
She swaddled them in grey leaves—
Sweet Mercy sister Dusk!

And Night the swarthy mother,
Drew on her sable glove—
Old night the foster Mother,
The screener o' light love!
Where never moon-beam ripples
Down hollow caves she crept,
And from the Earth's warm nipples,
Where clinging still they slept;

44

She drew each star-child glowing
And dewy from its nest,
The waking eyelids throwing
A halo on her breast;
And covering their faces,
Upon the pale moon bars,
By lone & secret places,
She mounted through the stars.

With holy dew to wet them,
And priestly Dark to shrive,
High o'er the South she set them,
The bright-eyed children Five.
And from a rocky highland,
Earth watched, till faint & far
Up in the distant sky-land
They opened star by star.

And night by night they grew there,
Till o'er the South Sea track
A blaze of light they threw there,
That reached the line & back;
And from lone bush-bound stations
To wild grey seas a-toss,
Men hail them from the Nations—
The Guide Lights of the Cross!

The Dream-Man

The stars in their helmets white
Keep guard o'er the sleeping towns,
With sabres all drawn & bright—
They watch for the Dream-Man's light,
That flits o'er the moonlit dawns.

Hark! is it a fairy lute
Just brushed by a night-bird's wing?
No sound but an owl's lone hoot—
The bush & her birds are mute;
But what do the star-winds sing?

Oh, what does the Dream-Man mean,
And why does he wave his wand?
Afar where the tussocks lean,
He walks on the plain unseen,
And calls to the night beyond.

The moon is be-ringed & pale,
And only the Dream-Man's eyes
May guide o'er the slender trail,
But what if their light should fail—
Away where the shadows rise?

He plays on a wond'rous reed,
And deep are the spells he weaves;
In vain may ye kneel & plead—
Who follows the Dream-Man's lead,
And falls by the way he leaves!

He tarries his steps for none;
But the gleam of his sombre eyes—
Oh, dearly their glance is won!
Is more than the stars & sun,
And all the light o' the skies.

Aloud from the distant sea,
And low from a far-off range,
He calls to the soul of me,
And plays in an unknown key
A song in a rhythm strange.

After the Storm

The wrinkled forehead of the sky
Doth chase the sunbeams as they fly,
  Like pale nuns in retreat;
Each drooping, half-averted eye,
   Wet-lashed with rain drops; and the sweet
Moist earth is surfeited:
A pale, weak invalid, the day,
Hath risen from her bed.

And I am tired & my brain
Is drowsed with murmur of the rain;
  Too dull am I for mirth,
Yet too indifferent for pain:
   The shadows ride upon the earth—
Grey pickets of the night,
That drive before them on the plain
The fugitives of light.

The Flame Flower [1]

A trailing, white wreath of clematis—
She comes—my fair Queen! & kind fate is
More free in her largesse to me.
Snow flowers, I'll twine you for Lee,
To crown the pale gold of her tresses,
Who shrinks from my burning caresses—
Aloof as a star in the sea.

Soft arms, dimpled arms, but they cling not;
Eyes promising passion they bring not,
Grey-green as the green of sea pools—
The fire that touches them cools;
But oh, for the rapture, the gladness—
One kiss, one wild clasp that were madness!
Well men are but lust-ridden fools.

I'll crown her with crown of bush flowers—
Wild sun bred & washed & spring showers,
Above the pale bloom of her face;
She leans in her sweetness & grace
From arms that are aching to hold her—
"Dear, rest your bright head on my shoulder—
Why, Lee, was I crushing your lace?"

First Night & the cellos are throbbing
To beat of the violins sobbing
About me the warm women glow
Eyes lustrous languid & slow
They pass me but thou art the fairest
As pure as the star-wreath thou wearest—
Mine Edelweiss, Flow'r of the snow!

"'Tis nothing, Lee—touch me, draw nearer—
Ah close, till my vision is clearer!"
A mirage burns into my brain,
Wild, memoried, leavened with pain:
Eyes down & her hands clasped before her—
Great God! do I loathe or adore her?
This phantom—this shade of Elaine.

Loose, gauzy light wrappings her limbs on,
Brave trappings of purple & crimson,
And gleaming white curve of her bust;
Like slender tree bowed in a gust,
She stands in the storm of their cheering,
Unheeding, unseeing, unhearing,
She—pap for them, Food for their lust!

This wreath of red rata I'll fling her,
Some dream of dead passion to bring her:
She sees it, her dark head is bowed,
The plaudits are ringing & loud.
Flame flowers flaring & scarlet,
Befitting the pomp of a harlot!
And—I—am but one of the crowd.

She—owned by the Lords of the high-ways—
Befouled in the slime of the by-ways,
A jibe for the tongues of the street;
(Ah, red lips so smiling & sweet!)
She stands like a wind-shaken flower
In pride of her passion & power,
The price of men's souls at her feet.

And she who was mine for the asking,
Who clung to me mutely unmasking—
She, spurned by a fool & a clown!
Ah, God! but a fold of her gown,
A fan she had played with were sweeter—
My eyes shall compel her, entreat her!
She sees me—the curtain is down.

*　　*　　*　　*　　*

"My head reels—a moment, Lee dearest,
Don take her—our carriage is nearest."
"For you, Sir: an answer to-night:"
"Val, meet me for old love's delight!"
I clench my hand closer, so that a
Crushed paper & spray of red rata
May lie in it hidden from sight.

The Flame Flower [2]

A trailing white wreath of clematis—
She comes—my fair Queen, & kind fate is
More free in her largesse to me.
Snow flowers, I'll twine you for Lee
To garland the gold of her tresses,
Who shrinks from my burning caresses,
Aloof as a star in the sea.

Fair arms, dimpled arms, but they cling not;
Eyes promising passion they bring not—
Grey green with the green of sea pools,
The fire that touches them cools.
But, oh, for the rapture, the gladness!
A kiss—a wild clasp that were madness—
We men are desire-driven fools!

I'll crown her with crown of wild flowers,
Sweet, sun-bred & culled from bush bowers,
Above the pale bloom of her face:
She leans in her languorous grace
From arms that are aching to hold her—
"Dear, rest your bright head on my shoulder.
Why, Lee, was I crushing your lace?"

*   *   *   *   *

Lights low & the cellos are throbbing
To beat of the violins sobbing;
About me the warm women glow—
Eyes lustrous languid & slow,
They pass me, but thou art the fairest,
As pure as the star-wreath thou wearest—
Mine edelweiss, flower of the snow!

"'Tis nothing, Lee, touch me—draw nearer—"
'Twill pass when my vision is clearer;
This fantasy, leavened with pain—
This mirage that burns in my brain:
Eyes down & her hands clasped before her—
Great God! do I loathe or adore her?
This painted, pale shade of Elaine.

Loose, gauzy, light wrappings her limbs on,
Brave trappings of purple & crimson,
And swan sweeping curve of her bust;
Like slender tree bowed in a gust,
She sways in the storm of their cheering,
Unheeding, unseeing, unhearing,
She—pap for them—Food for their lust!

This wreath of red rata I fling her,
A dream of dead passion to bring her—
She sees it, her dark head is bowed,
To plaudits far ringing & loud:
Flame flowers flaring & scarlet,
Befitting the pomp of a harlot!
And I—am but one of the crowd.

She, owned by the lords of the high-ways,
Befouled in the slime of the by-ways—
A jibe on the tongues of the street.
(Ah red lips so smiling & sweet!)
She stands like a wind-shaken flower,
In pride of her passion & power,
The price of men's souls at her feet.

And she who was mine for the asking,
Who clung to me mutely unmasking,
She—spurned by a fool & a clown!
Ah God! but a fold of her gown,
A fan she had played with were sweeter—
My eyes shall compel her, entreat her—
She sees me, the curtain is down.

*　　*　　*　　*　　*

"My head reels—one moment Lee, dearest—
Don take her; our carriage is nearest."
"For you, Sir: an answer to-night:"
"Val, meet me for old love's delight!"
I clench my hand closer, so that a
Crushed paper & spray of red rata
May lie in it hidden from sight.

Song of the Earth Spirit

When the light of the far heaven changes
        Through the day's broken bars,
O'er the peaks of the mystical ranges
        I arise with the stars;

And I pass in a wreath o' white vapour,
        When the shadows are done,
Where the arms of the sloping hills taper
        To the reach of the sun.

All the storm winds are huddled together,
        Crouching low in their lair—
Falls the down of a far eagle's feather,
        Like a stone in the air.

Oh, Beloved! my bosom is dreary
        As the lilt of a song,
When the heart of the singer is weary,
        And the rhythm is long.

Thy somnolent voice, as I listen,
        O'er the leagues of the turf,
Floats to me, & lo! thy limbs glisten
        On the crest of the surf.

Is there aught 'neath the wide sky's embowment,
      Like thy mighty unrest?
Oh, to lean for one lingering moment
      On thy turbulent breast!

How I long for thy waters to hold me,
      As they lap at my feet;
To flow over & fondle & fold me
      Till our joy be complete;

To inundate me, saturate, press me
      Over mountain & fen—
Oh arise in your strength & possess me
      From the cities of men!

The Storm Spirit

Free from their prison the storm-winds have burst
       In a galloping pack,
Foaming & loud over deserts of cloud,
Night like an outlaw flees hunted & curst—
       The hounds on her track.

What does it matter—the praise or the blame?
       Great souls of the past
That sculptured & wrought in the marble of thought,
Crowd in the darkness & call on my name
       Through lips of the blast.

Out where the wind seeketh sobbing & spent
       The lap of the plain;
Forms from the North rise & beckon me forth:
Vain would I seek them, but lo! they are bent
       Grey shapes of the rain!

Are they but shore—drift—the breath of the night
       And spume of the sea?
"Take up the cross of the longing & loss—"
Storm Fiend, speak! do I hear it aright?
       Thy message to me?

Driving the Cattle Home

Driving the cattle home,
  While the sun sits on the edge
Of the jagged hill as the shadows fill
  The curves of the mountain ledge—
  Driving the milch cows home.

See how the heifers creep,
  As they breast the wrestling tide,
And the clean flood swells to their clanging bells,
  A-wash on each branded side;
  Fording the Dead-Man's creek.

Whistle the collie Clown—
  (And this is the task he hates!)
"Heel the year-old steer away in the rear—"
  To the gates—the slip-rail gates—
  Lower the bar-gates down!

"See that the stalls are clear,
  And the pails in the milking shed.
She's a jade—the White, you can rope her tight;
  And the polly's loosed her head—
  Free of the bail-post here."

Driving the cattle home!
    For the stars are near the sky;
With a merry song as we move along,
    And the crawling mob goes by—
    Over the fields to home.

*　　*　　*　　*　　*

Pondering here I dream,
    Till the beach is white with foam,
And I hear the clang that the cowbells rang
    As we drove the cattle home.
    Forests the sea-plains seem,

Rolling in long grey lines:
    And the white-lipped wizards creep
From their unknown caves in the secret waves,
    And their foam steeds fall & leap
    Over the green-sea pines.

Stay till the mob goes by:—
    And the brown hides seamed and scarred,
From the long lean strip of the green-hide whip
    Hung up in the branding yard—
    Down where the yearlings cry.

There, where the sun rides low
    On the bend of Camel Peak—
Oh the tramp of hoofs & the station roofs!
    And the old wind on my cheek,
    Out where the light hearts go.

Driving the cattle home;
For the light is fading fast,
As they halting go with their heads hung low
Through the paddocks of the Past,
Over the years to home.

The Seed

In my heart's garden, overgrown,
The careless wind a stray seed planted:
It throve in dark dank mosses sown,
Where never ray of sunshine slanted.

And day by day I watched it grow,
While fell things sickened in their places;
Till blossoms dead long years ago
Reached up their pale & faded faces.

But soon a sullen wind that swept
And moaned around my secret bower,
Came peering through the leaves that kept
A screen about my stolen flower.

I covered it with weak decrial—
A worthless thing the breeze had tosst!
"In vain, oh Heart! is thy denial—
I seek a seed that I have lost."

No more its tendrils twine & cling,
Its buds the cruel wind hath looted;
A broken, soiled & ruined thing,
It lies upon my heart uprooted.

Oh, waste & bare & barren space!
Arise ye rank & bitter grasses,
And heal & cover o'er the place;
For pain must pass as passion passes.

The Body and Its Master

You that I deemed my sure asset,
    The bulwark of my will,
Have flouted me, but I am yet
    Inflexible & still.

And resolute & calm I wait;
    Obey weak trembling hands!
Be strong, imperative & straight,
    'Tis I—your Lord, commands.

Think not dim eyes that ache & burn,
    And brain that reels for rest,
To shake my purpose fixed & stern
    Or turn me from my quest.

Weak flesh that craves for false delights,
    I'll bend ye to my creed;
In days of toil & sleepless nights
    Ye shall forget your need.

I know upon the shining plain
    'Twere sweet to lie at ease,
With limbs relaxed & drowsing brain,
    To dream of heights like these;

Of sinews tense & sobbing breath
      And yawning chasms crost,
Where to the snowbound sleep were death,
      And rest a foothold lost.

But not for us the lotus grows—
      For us the ways are bleak,
And bound with ice & chilled with snows,
      And crowned by gleaming peak.

Baby's Sick

I've laid it all on Shamrock—
        Ten to one;
The knowing ones are backing
        Up old Sun.
I got a wire this morning—
        "Come home quick,
Mumma badly wants you—
        Baby's sick!"

The house is oddly quiet
        To my joy;
And yet I think I kind of
        Miss the boy!
His eyes are slow & heavy,
        Breathing quick;
His little pulse is flying—
        Baby's sick!

He couldn't eat his "plobob,"
        Wouldn't try
His "boom to bush the fobies
        Of the sky."
He's cast away his treasured
        Gee-gee stick—
No ride to-day to London;
        Baby's sick.

He scarce looks out the doorway,
                Nothing cares
For joys of alpine climbing
                On the chairs;
There lie his little shovel
                And his pick—
No need to watch the pathway!
                Baby's sick.

The house is up on tip-toes,
                Shadows creep
And crouch about in corners—
                He's asleep.
Don't let the news-boy wake him!
                Mabel quick
Run out & take the paper—
                Baby's sick.

Here's word about the races;
                Oh, I say!
The Sun has won the steeple—
                Second May.
Old Shamrock kicked the hurdle—
                Let him kick!
The Cup may go to—pieces!
                Baby's sick.

Songs of the Sluicers

By the Mouth of the Shaft

How the red light from the lant'rns
Lit the faces round the shaft,
Faces swarthy stern and tanned,
As they cut the fallen timber,
Cleared the rotten windlass aft—
Rigged another roughly planned.

One man fancied leaning over
Fastening on the jagged rope,
A faint movement in the brown,
Obscene ferment of the darkness;
Then Black Bill, the leader spoke:
"He's alive boys! Who'll go down?"

Pushing through the crowd that started,
Sam the Skiter forward sprung,
Caught the rope with steady hand,
"Lower down," he cried, "I'm ready!"
Round the creaking windlass swung—
Strained the rope in every strand.

Half-way down the foul air met him
And the candle flickered out,
Then the vapour seized his brain—
Clutched his throat with demon fingers,
But he raised a reeling shout,
And they hauled him up again.

"It's the gas mates! Where's the Tommy?
Cut those smoke bushes here—
Beat the air in, swirl 'em round—"
"Now let down a lighted candle:
Steady boy! the air is clear,"
And they wound him under ground.

With the fetid dark around him,
As the grinding windlass turned,
Till the vapour hung like smoke,
And the slinking shadows cowered,
Where the candle dimly burned,
Flickered on the straining rope.

Lit the damp & slimy shingles,
And the rotten beams abaft;
The lad felt a sudden chill,
He could hear the water dripping
From the mullock up the shaft
To the bottom black & still.

Down below him doubled under
'Neath a fallen mero trunk,
Something red and battered lay
Where the coil of stagnant water
Like a crawling viper slunk,
With its dazed & broken prey.

*   *   *   *   *

As they stood in silence round him,
One dark bearded digger spoke—
"Give him air. He's coming to!"
But the Skiter leaning over,
Shook his head, "Boys there's no hope!
See the lips are going blue."

And he raised him like a woman:—
"Ain't he altered as he lies
There so quiet like & strange—
A damned lump of mullock struck me
And the sands got in my eyes—
God! old fellow, what a change!

"And the girl at Riley's shanty—
We must break the blow to her,
They had fixed it up last week;
And he took this job prospectin'
The old workings on the spur,
For the lead of Golden Creek.

"Hurt her? Bless you! 'twon't much hurt her!
She'd hev chucked him for a kiss
From that measle of a toff,
Who some say—but nothing matters!
Poor old chap! he's come to this—
Boys the rain is keeping off;

"But the wind's from a bad quarter.
There's a brother; so I've heard,
But he hasn't wrote for years:
Send the yellow dust to Liza—
It was all she ever cared!
And she'll soon pan off her tears."

Then they laid him on a stretcher
With the night-wet on his hair,
And the blood-wet on his breast;
Harder weight than head of woman
That had pressed upon him there,
With the cross-beam on his chest!

Never more the quest of passion
With its raptures & alarms!
Never more for toil & graft:—
Had he thought of red lips clinging
And the circle of white arms,
As he stumbled on the shaft?

O'er the blue line of the ranges
Rose the dawning faint & chill,
And the moon a shadow dim,
Like a sorrow-stricken woman
Leaned her pale brow on the hill,
As the New Day broke for him.

A Deserted Diggings

The golden light is waning,
      Falling through
Yon sombre mountain gap;
O'er Mother Forest rolling
      Out of view;
The sleepy shadows gather
Low on her spacious lap.

The broad, grey flats are silent
      Blurred & dun;
About lie ruined huts,
Like dead men's bones a-bleaching
      In the sun;
Here runs an ancient truckway—
Hid in its grass-grown ruts.

It leads into a tunnel
      In the hill,
Where glow-worms gleam aloof;
And cobwebs bar the op'ning;
      All is still:
Like tears that follow laughter,
Drips water from the roof.

Nearby a rotten windlass
      Half o'ergrown
Lies ambushed in the flax;
A weka whistles shrilly
      From a lone
Log, in some faded summer
Felled by the ringing axe.

A dam is over yonder,
      Lying low
Behind its gravel banks,
Piled up by human labour
      Long ago;
The gauge is leaning over
Its water-sodden planks.

Like lepers, sad, forsaken
      Of their kind,
The pine tree's naked trunks
Arise, & from the stagnant
      Swamp behind,
Bereft & bare of branches
Reach up their withered stumps.

O'ergrown by matted bushes
      Is the race
Close by a ruined flume,
Where black pipes hissed the water
      On the "face,"
And swart & sweating sluicers
Drenched in the flying spume.

Here lies a rusty shovel,
             All about
Old boxes, rotten planks,
Just as the owners left them—
             "Duffered out!"
Oft have the blows of hammers
Rung on those rock-built banks.

Once down this silent gully,
             Laughter woke
The echoes of the gorge,
And from those ruined chimneys
             Issued smoke,
And loud the bellows panted
On yonder broken forge.

Oft round the camps at even'
             Tales were told,
And songs of many lands
Sung by the fire of rata;
             Miners old
Joined in the "Lang Syne" chorus,
And gripped each other's hands.

Where are ye now old comrades?
             Past alarms—
Past lust of gold or gilt!
The sinews of a nation
             In your arms,
Out of your strength & folly
A nation ye have built!

Two Nights

The hills were dark, as the star-crowned night
Flung swooning day from the mountain height,
    Where weary she crept to die;
The red blood streamed from her forehead white,
    And dripped on the twilight sky.

The darkness came like an evil thing
And sate. A hawk with a wounded wing
    Cried out from the lone bush bars:
The young moon dived in a golden ring
    To cover behind the stars.

And still—so still, that the pine trees heard
The quick heart-beat of a crouching bird,
    That cowered too faint for flight;
Like a whimpering babe a lost wind stirred
    And sank in the stagnant night.

A low, continuous, booming sound—
Like beat of surf on the distant Sound,
    It swelled in the rumbling east;
The deep hill heeled on the rolling ground
    And moaned like a waking beast.

The great earth strove & her anguish sealed,
She swayed & quivered but would not yield.
 As reeds in the wind bend nigh,
The staggering ranges round her reeled
 And toppled against the sky.

A rending shock & a fiery glow!
And oped the womb of the mountain slow
 With pains of a mighty birth;
That bent the walls of the world below
 The grip of the frenzied earth.

Flung hot & high from the flaming well
Hot showers of molten lava fell,
 And rocks in the lurid glare;
Belched the chasm of yawning hell
 Its spawn on the strangled air!

A deathly hush, & the boiling rill
That trickled out from the smoke-wreathed hill
 Crept over the blasted heath;
All save the wail of the wind was still,
 And moan of the earth beneath.

A sullen roar & a sheet of flame!
The mountain tottered & wrenched in twain,
 And blotting the stars' pale light,
The lava splattered with molten rain
 The eyes of the blinded night.

  * * * * *

The plains are dark: with her fingers deft
Dusk hides the seams that the chasms left
    Where the great hills sank from sight
And lofty brows of the range were cleft
    In wrath of that awful night!

The wild swans swim in a dark bayou
Where pines the trail of their shadows threw
    To snows on the mountain's bust
And out beyond where a forest grew
    Is lava & stones & dust

The bare hills ravished of fern & leaf,
Like strong men stand on their buried grief,
    Deep seared with the battle sign
Of here the cleft of a riven reef,
    Or trunk of a blasted pine.

The twisted shades of a goblin shape,
That dive & dance as the star-winds wake
    And crumple each dimpling wave—
The moonbeams know as they kiss the lake,
    It winds o'er a mountain's grave.

Love & Pain

Know ye not my name is Pain?
       I am Love's twin brother;
No art o' thine can break the chain
        That binds us to each other.

I let my brother lead the way,
       And then his keys I borrow—
Fond heart you oped to Love to-day—
       It may be Pain to-morrow!

The Half-Breed

Through the Heads in the blue heat haze,
Low, black hulks of the schooners glide—
Long white trails on the cloven tide—
Steering in to the gleaming bays.

Flecked with flame till they seem as one,
Domes & steeples & glist'ning spires
Cleave the smoke of a million fires,
Rising warm in the downing sun.

Crowds that sever & surge & meet—
Crowds that clamour & sound along,
Like the lilt of a blind-man's song
Falls the beat of their drifting feet.

Up the Strand where the white girls go,
Down the lanes where the Half-Breeds play—
White & yellow, yellow & grey—
One there creeps like a shade of woe.

City, see where the Half-Breed stands:
Vain the guns at your harbour mouth!
Spawn o' the East & the hot red South
Holds your heart in her unclean hands.

Fetid foul to the sweet-breathed sea
Blows the blast from her burning lips
Floating out to the anchored ships
Drifting down on the winding Quay.

Sears the kiss of her loathsome mouth—
Spreads the blight of her poisoned veins,
Gorged & full with the blood she drains;
Ah the blood of the fresh young South!

The Summons of the Winds

Brave winds, be the sport of my mirth—
Ye slaves of me—Spirit of Earth!
When Chaos deposed & unseeing
Alone in the darkness was fleeing,
And matter was called into being,
I quickened, the Spirit of Earth.

Ha! Mortals 'tis me whom ye dread!
The mountains quake under my tread,
I laugh as I rend them asunder,
And drag them to furnaces under;
Men's cities I ravage & plunder,
And nourish my soul with their dead.

Blow over me Winds of the Earth,
Who muttered & sighed at my birth:
Come up from the sunsets far glowing
O'er oceans where salt spray is blowing,
From ice-bergs where grey clouds are snowing—
Draw round me ye, Winds of the Earth!

Chorus of the Winds

We have swept o'er the frozen Antarctic,
Floated o'er the ice-bounded Arctic
       From the poles of the earth;
From our play in the keel-ripped Atlantic,
We have hastened all furious & frantic
       From the midst of our mirth;
And the labouring frenzied Pacific
That we left in the travail terrific
       Of a mad tempest's birth;
We have passed where the planter was sowing,
Over plains with the sugar-cane growing
       By the globe's torrid girth;
O'er the wastes of Barren we whirlèd,
Where red sands of the desert are swirlèd
       In the simoom's hot breath:
Over battlefields crimson with corses,
Lying stark by the trunks of their horses,
       And the guns spitting death:
We have cooled with the balm of our lotion
Cities fevered with lust & emotion—
From the land & the air & the ocean,
       At your call we assemble
       Oh, Spirit of Earth!

Helblatavesky's Cow

'Twas up in Sandy's Gully 'mid Britishers in shoals,
A score or two of pig-tails & squads of German Poles,
I met Helblatavesky—his name he never got;
For when we cut it shorter we only made it hot—
That's how he got Equator. When Peter counts the sins
Writ in the book of Sandy's, he'll find the tale begins
When 'Quator brought a frowsy, lean, shambling little, brown
Cow up to decent Sandy's—the peaceful little town!
She ate our shirts & flannels, our gumboots & our socks,
'Twas in the age of canvas with neither bars nor locks.
Tom Rudd had lost his collar & eighteen carat stud,
And Tracy's best suspenders—she chewed them in her cud.
We'd had a decent washin' an' as I bossed the show
They'd left it in my keepin'—Equator Frank & Co.
But as the chows were swarmin' as thick as hivin' ants.
I took the stuff & sewed it inside my winter pants.
A day or two soon after Equator slouched around,
He'd got it in his fat head to take the gold to town:
"My poy it will be safer:" I turned to reach the moles.
And, gad! a fantail's feather'd hev knocked me off my poles!
In vain I groped & hunted, Equator looking on
At me half-dazed & flustered: "Old man the beans are gone!"
"De peans? I onderstan' not! Vot peans? 'Tis gold I vant—
My hard earn lofely money dat you have in your pant!"
"You go—" I said—exact. "your—" I called her something bad—
"Old cow has scoffed my breeches, & gold as well, by gad!"
"My cow," he shrieked, "you robber! you teef—you Breetish skunk

84

You tink me mad or silly? My cow steal from your bunk?"
By this a crowd was round us, my mates were looking grim
"Here, make the dog confess it, or break his head for him!"
"His neck you mean," cried Slippem, the new chum from the States
"String up the dirty spieler, who'd try to rob his mates!"
'Twas short but very lively; the tent was like a wreck,
And me hauled in the open a rope about my neck.
They soon fixed up the trial; a jury was enrolled;
The judge was old Equator who raved about his gold.
I waited for the verdict—it seemed for years & years,
When loud a high-pitched bellow came rumblin' in my ears:
As 'Quator bent to ask 'em if they was all agreed,
"Hold on" I cried, "you scrubbers—my counsel's come to plead!"
The old cow came upon us as hard as she could tear
A-down the rollin' terrace her tail high in the air,
No leg-rope could have stopped her—for Law she didn't reck,
She reared upon her haunches her hoofs about my neck!
"The old cow's off her onion!" "She's something on her mind."
"Perhaps she's feeling poorly, an' going to be confined!"
Said Tracy, "She's the culprit, I wouldn't mind to bet;
So cheer up, Tom, old fellow, you're on your kickers yet!"
At this the old gel bellowed, a-holdin' up for proof
A shred of tattered trousers a-sticken to her hoof,
She waved it in our faces—I tremblin' like a leaf—
That half-digested mole-skin, the rag of my reprieve!
"Old man we've been too hasty—we're sorry from our souls!
Best hanty round the hat boys; git Tom a pair of moles,
As sort o' compensation," 'Twas Silas Slippem spoke—
He who had been so forred in fixin' up the rope.
"But what about the prisoner—the gold thief," said Tom Rudd,

"I guess we'd best prospect her!" (a-thinkin of his stud.)
But I swore I'd protect her who gamely stood by me
And drove her round the tailin's & milked in time for tea
She nearly filled the bucket with milk so awful thick,
We took the cream upon it & broke it with a pick;
And shortly after teatime when cook was washin' up
He panned a fairish prospec' from out the 'namelled cup.
But as she got dyspeptic an' long an' lean an' lank,
And never paid a divy, we christened her the Bank.
One day as she stood dozin' & flickin' off the flies,
I fancied she looked bilious & yellow round the eyes,
And brought for a tit-bit an' old-gum water-tight—
A little snack for supper, to tempt her appetite;
When early the next morning I carried in her chaff,
S'help me, my Colonial! she'd calved a Golden Calf!

Laura's Holiday

When Laura from the city gay
      Came out to Whitom Gorge,
To spend her summer holiday
      With Babs & Cousin George;
She found our nights were rather dry—
      The city sights she missed;
So on one luckless evening I
      Engaged to teach her whist.

And Laura quickly learnt to play,
      With arch exultant face,
Whene'er he looked another way
      She'd trump her partner's ace;
And diamonds he might lead to her—
      And diamonds trumps to boot,
But if he played his heart to her,
      She'd never follow suit.

Now all went well till from the yards
      Came handsome stockman Jim
And then she tired of playing cards
      And rode about with him
She cracked a whip with graceful turn
      For Laura played to win
And soon she thought she'd love to learn
      To round the cattle in.

So out she went one sunny morn
        Well mounted on a grey,
She drove the cattle by the barn
        That held the winter's hay:
The station mob was rather tame—
        The gates were open wide,
They seemed to understand the game,
        And soon they were inside.

They raided all the winter's hay
        And tramped the turnips down,
They broke the garden rails away—
        And blessed the girl from town!
That night the station owner raved,
        "'Twas wicked," Laura said,
She feared he never would be saved,
        Such sinful words he said.

'Twas wondrous how the shingles kept
        The roof from falling in!
And from her window Laura wept
        Adieu to stockman Jim.
Now one day to the station came
        A sportsman all alone;
They told him there was whips of game—
        There was—if he had known!

And Laura from her garden seat
        Had spied him riding down—
She *was* so very glad to meet
        With someone from the town!
He wore a natty riding suit,
        And drawled his words a bit:
'Twas strange she'd always wished to shoot—
        Did she—aw—could she hit?

Next day they got the rifle out
        And rammed the bullet home,
Then took an old tin-teapot spout
        And stuck it on a stone.
He said she held the gun too slack—
        She thought he was a brute,
And when he dodged behind her back,
        She vowed she wouldn't shoot.

He'd have to come & stand right out
        While she took careful aim,
He needn't think she'd miss the spout—
        She understood the game!
She swayed in most unnerving guise,
        The gun was wobbling round;
She pulled the trigger—shut her eyes,
        And dropped it on the ground.

Alas! the bullet fired astray—
        It never touched the mark,
But on the ground the sportsman lay
        She'd stretched him stiff & stark.
And when into the nearest shed
        The bleeding youth they bore,
She said she hoped he wasn't dead—
        She'd never missed before.

'Twas all the gun—how could she aim
        A shot with such a thing?
That gunsmith didn't know the game
        Of manufacturing!
The doctor said: "He'll not depart;
        The thing was neatly done,
The bullet flirted by his heart
        And settled in his lung.

"Foul play? Oh, well, you needn't tell.
        Whoever took the aim,
You bet he knew his business well—
        He understood the game!
He'll get about? yes—by & by—
        Say in six months or more;"
And Laura said that she could cry
        And asked him was it sore.

But still he really must rejoice;
>> The pain would soon abate—
The patient lifted up his voice,
>> And swore with feeble hate.

And Laura heard with pained surprise;
>> 'Mid chill & frigid hush,
She said she thought it would be wise
>> To pack & leave the bush.
If Cousin George & Babs felt bad
>> They showed themselves resigned
They harnessed Bob & roused the lad
>> In case she'd change her mind.

So off she set when daylight came:
>> "Folks up at Whitom Gorge
Don't seem to understand a game,"
>> She told her Cousin George;
But still with hope his bosom buoyed—
>> She'd come again some day;
Because she really had enjoyed
>> Her little Holiday!

Humorous Verse

The Chronicles of Sandy Gully
as Kept by Skiting Bill

"The sandy pug was risin' an' the claim was duffered out,
The divy of the washin' wouldn't pay a three bob shout;
We 'greed we'd have to chuck it, an' ses Bill, "let it be soon,"
A-strollin' round the town-ship one Sunday afternoon.
A city bloke came by us, his nose stuck in the air,
A forty acre shirt front, & ile upon his hair;
He spoke up pretty sociable & open like & free;
He was a minin' expert, so he said to Bill & me,
A travlin' fur a syndicate an' jus' come up on spec—
He sorter eased the collar a-scrapin' on his neck.
We talked a little further, an' I got my lamps on Bill,
And took the new chum expert by the short cut up the hill
To see our minin' proputy. He hemmed a bit,
And fondled with his eyeglass & said he'd think of it;
But first he'd try a prospec'; Bill he turned as pale as chalk,
He said that it was Sunday—the other chaps might talk
At breakin' of the Sabbath, but if he would come next day
And try a dozen dishes, he'd find the thing would pay!
At dark that night we fixed it, & I doctored up the pug,
Touched all the lightly places. "He is just a toffish mug
'Twill learn him some of business if it takes him down a cut,"
And then we slep' like children in our 'umble little 'ut.
Next mornin' in the paddock when the toff had washed a dish,
He sunk upon the barrer lookin' like a dyin' fish!
"'Tis reelly most surprisin'! you hev struck the golden lead—

We'll float it in a company if you are both agreed?"
An' so we made it over to—he said his name was Snares—
For cash down fifteen hundred, & a thousand paid up shares—
"Of course when it is floated—why what the dooce is this?"
(He stumbled on the nugget that we got at Coolabis.)
'Twas over fifty ounces & a pretty bit o' quartz,
The gold a-stickin' on it like a little bunch o' wartz.
"'Twill do; a fairish sample; I will take it up to town—
They mightn't know of Sandy's—you can get it when you're down.
The shares'll go like pasties; for there are no flies on this!"
(He carried off the nugget that we got at Coolabis.)
I shouted down at Reilly's & we wet the golden sell;
The expert named it handsome by a name we couldn't spell;
"Te Katipo Extended," he said softly, "by your leave;
It means a little spider that does a little weave.
May it prove a money weaver! Haw—a pint of orange fizz.
Now boys fill up your glasses & drink success to biz!"
"Oh, raise me up," ses William, when the toff had said good-by
He walked into that cobweb—"Lord he's just a little fly!"
We watched the post like lovers,—we could 'ardly eat or sleep;
And got a lot o' paper from the expert in a week.
"Te Katipo Extended": it looked flourishin' & fine;
But 'bout the fifteen hundred he never dropped a line.
Then I got sort o' restless and Bill was mooching roun'
Alone some for the nugget; so we took a trip to town
We struck the minin' expert a-walkin' with a girl
He said he'd see us private as he gave his cane a twirl
Sez Bill: "We've come from Sandy's, and we're not to be put off—
Hand up that fifteen hundred!" Well you should ha' seen the toff
He cocked his little eyeglass, & sez he, "You must forget!

We 'greed to stand that over—it is in the claim as yet,
Which judgin' from the prospec's will pay nigh a thousand pound
A week. You'll get your divy in the first wash from the ground!"
"What's left for us, the owners, will you tell us Mr. Snares?"
He murmured out politely, "You have got the paid-up shares!"
Bill was rollin' up his shirt-sleeves, but I didn't want no hits:
"Here, chuck us back our sample & we'll cry that we are quits—
Give up our bloomin' nugget & take back the paid up shares!"
He said, "You're very foolish; for I am S. P. Snares
The well known minin' expert, & you are Tom & Bill—
Two of the biggest rascals that loaf at Sandy Hill;
Take a friend's advice you'd better—" then he stopped to parry Bill;
I rushed him in the rearward—Oh! he wanted all his skill.
A crash, & all the atmosphere was red & green & blue!
I sittin' in the gutter, was the next thing that I knew,
And Bill a-lyin' near me; but we saw no more of Snares
The week we stopped in city to undergo repairs
I'd swallowed half my molars, & Bill had lost an eye,
But never touched the expert, who was "just a little fly."

A Song of the Hills

Glowing noon on spire & steeple—
Never boon of shadow spun
O'er the parched ways for the people,
In this City of the Sun.
Through the glaring day I sicken for the purple on the Hills—
For the storm-light on the peaks,
When the mighty thunder speaks,
And the tearing torrents quicken in the wide womb of the Hills.

Is it strife for place & plunder?
Or the glory of the quest?
When the weaklings stumble under,
Shall I fall among the rest?
And I reel amid the riot of the never-resting mills,
Where the ground & garnered grains
Are the spoil of human brains,
Till I hunger for the quiet of the strong & silent Hills.

From the crowd's incessant motion,
And the feud 'twixt faith & creed—
Oh, for some magician's potion!
Like the ancient charms we read,
That might bear me from men's babble to the cloisters of the Hills,
Like pale friars grouped around
Keeping guard on holy ground,
Where the stooping branches dabble in a cool-lake in the Hills.

Old Tuhua's grey form ending
Where the lake & mountain meet,
Like Achilles, stern, unbending,
With dead Hector at his feet.
Are there smouldering desires in the sombre Stoic Hills?
Hidden craters in the deeps
Of their chill & frozen steeps—
Are there wells of molten fire in the shut hearts of the Hills?

And I feel the undulating
Of a chord invisible—
All my spirit palpitating
With a strange magnetic thrill;
And I may not stay nor falter; for it draws me where it wills:
'Tis the wand the Magi wields
O'er his vast & icy fields,
From a dim untapered altar in the circle of the Hills.

The Call of the Dream Man

'Twas a voice in the darkness calling—
    I heard & I dared not stay;
Though as faint as a white star falling
    Afar from the Milky Way,
Was the glimmering light he carried,
    And never a moon to guide.
Oh, I knew that the Dream Man tarried
    For none on the way beside!

As we entered the sombre forest,
    All sensitive, shrinking things
That the stare of the sun abhorest,
    Hid under the brooding wings
Of the sheltering dark, to meet me
    Came forth in the still star-shine;
For the Mother Bush bent to greet me,
    And gave me the secret sign.

Of the pass to her obscure places
    And wondrous things behind,
I was free of her great green spaces,
    And free of the moon & wind;
For they taught me the words they uttered
    In mystical unknown tongue;
Till I knew what the rain drops muttered
    The pattering leaves among.

But a moon flower wreath to weave me
   I lagged at my lover's door;
And the Dream Man turned to leave me
   As those he had left before.
"For the rapture of soft endearment
   Were more to thy life's behove,"
But I clung to his trailing cerement
   "O, Master, I only love!"

And I passed from my heart's desire,
   And followed him through the night,
Till he breathed in words of fire—
   "Go sing of thy love aright!"

The Last Lover

"I thirst, my Love! Let the warm blood flow
Until thy turbulent veins are dry.
Red roses lie on the heart I covet,
As strong wine splashes the lips that love it;
To pledge thee here where the deep drops glow,
I hasten, love; for I heard thy cry.

"What staunchest thou with thy fingers slight?
That runneth o'er on thy warm, wet breast—
Strange sap to flow from a milk white bosom!
And ravest thou in thy grief to lose him?
Who caged a bird for his sole delight,
To fling it forth from a rifled nest.

"And one who lovèd thee passing well—
For whom a strand of thy glist'ning hair
Were bond enow! in thy pride forsaken,
He sleeps too deep at thy need to waken,
Who would have sat by the bars of hell
To hold thy hand for a moment there.

"He spurred his steed till its flanks were dyed
And deep chest labouring brokenly
A demon chaunt in the frenzied rhythm,
Of pounding hoofs on the plain went with him;
Was thine the fault when the gelding shied,
And flung him prone on a fallen tree?

"One knelt by thy pillow passion pale,
Who fled away through the midnight dim—
Dost thou remember the lonely waking?
To moaning surf on the low rocks breaking
And white sea foam in the schooner's trail?
Now nought it matters to thee or him!

"One stooped to fondle a fallen rose
Dropt from a fold on thy scented gown;
Now crushed & low in the dust it lieth,
For other rose than thy rose he sigheth—
A bud that odorous crimson grows,
And thine is gathered & soiled & brown.

"With two white passion flowers on thy face—
Meet blossoms these for our bridal bed!
May shrink not, sweet, while thy limbs I cover—
No shame should lie between loved & lover:
And priests shall mumble above the place,
Wherein we two take our joy," Death said.

The Magic Island

Not a wind o'er the still Pacific, not a light on the dreaming bay
Save the tapers the star-men carry as they follow the bier of day.
And I crouch in the night concealèd that the mad mothers may not hear
What the murmuring sea-shell whispers, as I hold it against mine ear;
For it tells me a wondrous story that only the Mermen know,
And the souls of the little children who are drowned in the pools below.

But the mothers are always listening—that they haply may understand,
To the tales that the shells are telling to each other upon the sand:
And they grasp at the mystic meaning, as a child at a dancing beam
When it dapples the beach a moment in its play on a darkened stream.
And the babbling sea-shell murmurs with its lips to my eager ear—
Very close, for the mothers listen—very low, lest the waves might hear:

"In a moon in the far-off ages 'neath the glitter of stars like these,
Like the waste of a leafless garden lay the leagues of the lone South Seas;
Till the Grey Wizard to the Ocean said: 'Oh! barren thy fields and bare
Is the reach of thy rolling acres—I shall plant me an Island there.'
And the veins of her throbbed and quivered with the pulse of a life to be,
As the seed of the Wizard quickened in the womb of the desert sea.

"And it throve in the great Pacific, till the hills of it peak by peak,
Like the leaves of a flower unfolded from the soil of the untilled deep.
And 'twas thus in the distant ages that the chattering sea-fowl flew
O'er the shores of the magic Island, as out of the waves it grew.
Said the Grey Wizard to the Ocean: 'It is far from the prying ken
Of the tribes of the mean Earth people, of the race of the pigmy men,
Who would plunder her woods for cities and for ships with their merchandise;'
But the men of the Earth are cunning though they may not be overwise.

"So they built them a fair great galley where the bergs of the North Sea toss,
And they steered for the mystic Island by the light of a strange White Cross.
Till they swarmed on her shining beaches as an eagle swoops on a crag;
And they builded a spacious city 'neath the flaunt of a flaring flag.
But the children came from the galley and the Grey Wizard watched their play,
As they paddled among the shallows in the sands of a golden bay;
Until into the deep he lured them by the craft of the sly green waves;
With sinuous seaweed bound them in the slime of the unsunned caves.

"But the little Earth men are valiant and they followed the children's track;
Laughed the Grey Wizard in the breakers, as he baffled and hurled them back.
Loud he scoffed at the weak white swimmers, for he swam as a sea-god swims,
And he marked how they stained the billows as he scattered their puny limbs.
And the wailing of women reached him as he sat where the waters glide,
As he dozed like a demon sated on the lap of the dipping tide.

"But some night in the unborn ages in a mystical moon to be,
Shall the beautiful Island vanish in the depths of the desert sea;
And the mothers shall reach their kingdom when the sea hath her own again,
And the Grey Wizard takes his treasure from the tribes of the pigmy men."
And this is the wondrous story murmured into my eager ear:
Very close—lest the Wizard listen, very low, for the waves might hear.

And I whisper it to the mothers as they roam by the booming bars,
Till their hollow eyes gleam and glisten with a light that shall reach the stars.
For 'tis not but the sheen of waters that they see when the sunsets flare,
But the locks of the little children and their glittering wave-wet hair;
And 'tis not but the stars' reflection that they see when the sunset cools
But the eyes of the little children that are drowned in the green sea pools.

Notes on the Poems

This volume is based on the 1905 typescript in the Mitchell Library. The typescript has holograph notations and revisions in pencil. Many of the annotations match those made on other manuscripts in the Stephens' collection in the Mitchell Library. Since the vast majority of the revisions correct obvious typos and errors, those revisions have been incorporated into the edition here. Some of the revisions may very well have been in Lola Ridge's hand but are most probably Stephens'. (It should be noted that editors would, in the custom of that period, alter authors' texts at will, often without permission. This practice was especially true of male editors working on texts written by female authors.) If there were any corrections to the typescript for misspellings (British standard) or other punctuation and grammatical errors, they have been corrected and the corrections listed in the individual notes on the poems below. While British standard spellings have been retained, usage of single and double quotes follows American practice since Ridge used both in the typescript, but primarily adopted American standard usage. Ridge was also inconsistent in her usage of capitalization and punctuation. For this edition, effort was made to make her capitalization consistent within a poem but not from poem to poem. Her punctuation has mostly been retained, corrected in only instances of egregious errors or for clarity. On some pages of the typescript there are lines of spaced dots across the page. There is no conclusive evidence as to what these lines of dots represented. They have been retained here as a row of centered asterisks. The notes also contain any information on other publications of the poems, any notable differences with the periodical version and explanations of specific terms not common knowledge outside of Australasia. When available, the periodical publication of a poem was used to resolve any questions in the typescript.

Under Song. Line 2: Deep throated. Line 14: birds. Published in *Overland Monthly* (June 1908): 540. Same text, copy edited; and in *The Ghetto and Other Poems* 1918: 95–96. "Under-Song." Rewritten.

At Sun-Down. Line 1: bush. Line 7: A rātā is a tree native to New Zealand with bright red flowers, hard dark red wood and dark green leaves. Line 8: gallexys. Line 22: turbulant. Line 25: forfiet. Line 30: bush. Published in the *Bulletin*, Sept. 10, 1903: 16. Titled "At Sundown."

Dawn on the Mountains. Line 20: A rātā is a New Zealand tree with bright red flowers, dark red wood and dark green leaves. Line 30: No indent in typescript. Line 37: closéd. Line 39: composéd. Published in *Otago Witness*, Apr. 23, 1902: 59.

Lake Kanieri. Line 4: Mt. Tūhua is near Lake Kaniere in Westland. Line 8: Insistant. Line 14: rythmic. Line 18: after glow. Line 20: clamor. Published in *New Zealand Illustrated Magazine*, Nov. 1902: 131. In Ridge's time, the town and lake were spelled Kanieri. Kaniere is the modern spelling.

The Bush. Line 11: Each wistful glances. Line 12: a-loof. Line 21: un-quiet. Published in *Bulletin*, Sept. 29, 1904: 16. Omits second stanza and has line 11 as "Each, wistful, glances like a lover back" and with line 33 as "Go, learn and listen at her mother knee." Published in *Gunter's Magazine*, July 1910: 45. And published in *The Lone Hand*, Dec. 1, 1908: 176–78.

Dead-Pine Shadows. Title: Dead Pine. Published in *New Zealand Illustrated Magazine*, May 1903: 140.

The Hour of Dawn. Line 4: half shut. Line 17: premanted. Line 23: sicken. Published in *Bulletin*, Jun. 15, 1905: 3.

On the Track. Line 3: places. Line 19: Jar. Line 20: sunbeams. Line 21: spangel. Published in *Bulletin*, Oct. 1, 1903: 16.

Think of Me Not With Sadness. Line 7: sorce. Line 21: A kauri is a coniferous tree found in New Zealand. Published as "Parted," in the *Bulletin*, Apr. 19, 1906: 40. Major revisions; contains speaker identification and a man's reply not in the typescript version.

To an Old Playfellow. Line 2: A rātā is a tree native to New Zealand with bright red flowers, hard dark red wood and dark green leaves. Line 4: A kauri is a coniferous tree found in New Zealand. Lines 5 & 25: Tutu is a poisonous shrub native to New Zealand. Line 6: o'er grown. Line 8: Bunyup. A bunyip is a mythical Australian freshwater monster. The stone may be a local landmark on or near a river (possibly made up by Ridge). Line 15: A tūī is an endemic passerine bird of New Zealand. Line 15: A miro (modern spelling) is a tree native to New Zealand. Line 16: locusts. Line 18: souls. Line 19: t'was. Line 28: Slight indent. Line 29: mistical. Line 31: highway. Published in the *Bulletin*, May 3, 1906: 35.

The Summons. Line 1: North-wind. Line 11: persistant. Line 13: tone? Line 14: insistant.

The Three Little Children. Line 5: gumtree. Line 6: follow-ed. Line 7: grass sown. Line 14: A free selector is roughly equivalent to a homesteader. Line 20: rain wet. Published in the *Bulletin*, March 15, 1902: 36. Children unnamed and no gender distinctions.

The Incurable. Line 2: out. Line 8: South. Lines 25 & 33: dead-house. Line 35: sun-beam. Published in the *Bulletin*, Nov. 29, 1902: 3.

When the Moon Was in Eclipse. Line 22: greydowns. Line 37: hatered. Line 41: & pain. Line 44: sillie. Line 78: jewel spanned. Published in the *Bulletin*, July 20, 1905: 39.

Moon-Struck. Line 9: skys. Line 20: white faced. Line 22: But. Reminiscent of "The Ghetto": 'The moon, blond and burning, creeping to their cots / Softly, as on naked feet. . . / Lolling on the coverlet. . . like a woman offering her white body. // Nude glory of the moon!' Published as "Moonstruck" in *New Zealand Illustrated Magazine*, Jan. 1904: 271.

My Care. Line 2: flung back. Line 8: gumtrees. Published in *Ainslee's Magazine*, March 1920: 83. Revised.

Song of the Earth. Line 2: days. Line 3: mistical. Line 16: rythm. Line 21: ought. Line 24: turbulant. Holograph note on typescript: "See page 47" [poem is on typescript pages 27–28]. Revised as "Song of the Earth Spirit" on typescript pages 47 and 48 (book page 55 here). Typed note on typescript page 48: "I revised these pieces last night & as they seem to sound better am sending you the copy." Published in the *Bulletin*, Nov. 16, 1905: 40. Under title of "The Song of the Earth Spirit" and with only seven stanzas (last one dropped). Also see, "After Storm" in *Sun-Up and Other Poems*: 'an eagle's feather / might fall like a stone." Published as "Song of the Mist," in *Gunter's Magazine*, March 1910: 39.

Forgive dear heart. . . . Line 11: flys. . . skys. Published as "Beth," in *Australian Town and Country Journal*, July 26, 1905: 28. Only second and third stanzas. Also published as "Beth" in *Gunter's Magazine*, May 1909: 506.

The Parting. Line 4: bitter sweet. Line 13: possums.

On Zealandia. Line 11: skys. Line 13: thats. Line 27: Battalian. Published as "On Zelanda," in *Canterbury Times*, Aug. 25, 1892: 33.

Sleep Dolores. Throughout the poem the Mitchell manuscript typist has typed Dolorias, including in the title. Given that the poem was published in the *Bulletin* under the title "Sleep, Dolores" and a related section exists in "Sun-Up" with the line "Oh for the light of thine eyes Dolores," this might be an instance of the typist's consistent errors in interpreting Lola's handwriting. Line 10: Deep. Line 20: Night-coast. Line 36: Added close quote at end. Published in the *Bulletin*, July 7, 1904: 3.

The Legend of the Cross. Line 3: earth. Line 19: layden. Line 20: Daised. Line 36: ariel. Line 48: high born. Line 51: farie's. Line 93: bush bound. Published in *New Zealand Illustrated Magazine*, April 1903: 45–46.

The Dream-Man. Title: Dream Man. Line 10: star winds. Line 13: A-far. Line 30: skys. Line 35: rythm. Published in *New Zealand Illustrated Maga-*

zine, Dec. 1903: 247; and in *Ainslee's*, Apr. 1909: 120. Revised later in the lost *Verses* typescript.

After the Storm. Line 5: wet lashed. Line 11: No indent. Line 13: No indent. Published in the *Bulletin*, Jan. 5, 1905: 3.

The Flame Flower [1]. The manuscript page has a circled 1 written over the title to signify first version (typescript pages 41–43). Line 1: wreathe. Line 14: lust ridden. Line 20: Dear rest. Line 25: lusterous. Line 32: levened. Lines 43 & 69: A rātā is a New Zealand tree with bright red flowers, dark red wood and dark green leaves. Line 51: byways. Line 58: un-masking. Line 62: compell.

The Flame Flower [2]. The manuscript page has a circled 2 written over the title to signify the revised version (typescript pages 44–46). Line 14: desire driven. Line 18: langerous. Line 25: lusterous. Line 31: levened. Lines 43 & 69: A rātā is a New Zealand tree with bright red flowers, dark red wood and dark green leaves. Line 45: see. Line 62: compell. Line 67: loves.

Song of the Earth Spirit. Line 5: wreathe. Line 11: eagles. Line 16: rythm. Line 21: ought. On the typescript page there is this typed note at the end of the poem: "I revised these pieces last night & as they seem to sound better am sending you the copy." On page 34 here in this book "Song of the Earth" represents an earlier version, which this poem might replace. Published in the *Bulletin*, Nov. 16, 1905: 40. Seven stanzas (last stanza dropped). Also see, "After Storm" in *Sun-Up and Other Poems*: "an eagle's feather / might fall like a stone."

The Storm Spirit. Line 8: sculptored. Appeared in the *Bulletin*, Feb. 9, 1905: 3. Titled "Storm Spirit."

Driving the Cattle Home. Line 32: white lipped. Published in *Otago Witness*, March 12, 1902: 59; and in *New Story Magazine*, Sep. 1911: 128.

The Seed. Line 1: over grown. Published in *Australian Town and Country Journal*, May 17, 1905: 35.

The Body and Its Master. Line 26: No indent. Line 28: No indent. Published in *Australian Town and Country Journal*, Aug. 9, 1905: 22.

Baby's Sick. Line 1: shamrock. Line 17: plobob is porridge. Line 19: means "broom to brush the cobwebs." Line 22: gee-gee is Australian slang for horse; hobby-horse is meant here. Line 23: to day. Published in the *Bulletin*, July 30, 1903: 3. Without baby-talk.

Waiting. In the typescript, the "Contents," or more correctly an index of first lines, lists a poem entitled "Waiting" on typescript pages 56 & 57.

However, those pages in the typescript are missing and the title of the poem on the index page is crossed out. It should be noted that this poem is included in Ridge's revised typescript, but copies of those pages are not available. Published in *Bulletin*, Jan. 28, 1904: 3.

By the Mouth of the Shaft. In the typescript index (Contents) this poem is listed by the section name "Songs of the Sluicers." Line 14: A skite is slang for a boaster. Line 19: Half way. Line 25: Its. Line 26: moka. Lines 41 & 58: mullick. A mullock is waste rock from mining. Line 44: A miro (modern spelling) is a tree native to New Zealand. Line 51: too. Line 56: Aint. Line 73: winds. Line 75: has'n't. Line 94: sorrow stricken. Published in the *Bulletin*, Nov. 23, 1901: 3.

A Deserted Diggings. Line 11: mens. Line 14: grass grown. Line 17: a-loof. Line 23: o'er grown. Line 25: A weka is a large flightless New Zealand rail. Line 35: water sodden. Line 43: O'er grown. Line 49: Slight indent. Line 67: A rātā is a New Zealand tree with bright red flowers, dark red wood and dark green leaves. Published in *Bulletin*, Oct. 5, 1901: 3. Titled "A Deserted Diggings: Maoriland."

Two Nights. Line 1: star crowned. . . Night. Line 11: pinetrees. Line 21: Earth. Line 33: No indent. Line 35: No indent. Line 43: stars. Line 65: mountains. Published in *Canterbury Times*, March 9, 1893: 43. This and the next six poems do not seem to fit into the section heading "Songs of the Sluicers." It is not known whether Stephens or Ridge were responsible for the manuscript's organization, and whether the typescript reflects a structuring in process.

Love & Pain. Published in the *Bulletin*, Oct. 22, 1903: 13. Revision in last line. See pages xxii–xxiii here for the *Bulletin* version. And published as "Love and Pain" in *Gunter's Magazine*, Jan. 1910: 179.

The Half-Breed. Line 10. clamor. Published in the *Bulletin*, Aug. 26, 1904: 3.

Chorus of the Winds. Line 1: Antartic. Line 2: Artic. Line 8: Best reading of "travail" since it appears the "ai" is inserted in handwriting over the typescript. Line 9: tempests. Line 13: whirléd. Line 14: swirléd. Line 15: A simoom is a hot, dusty desert wind. Line 16: battle fields. Line 18: splitting. Published in *Gunter's Magazine*, Jun 1909: 800.

Helblatavesky's Cow. Line 6: tail. In terms of meaning, "tale" might be preferred, but "tail" provides a broader pun. Line 9: flannels our. Line 10: canvass. Line 16: sowed. Line 20: A fantail (pīwakawaka) is a small native New Zealand bird. Line 22: half dazed. Line 28: sillie. Line 35: en-rolled. Line 38: high pitched. Line 39: a-greed. Line 47: "she's. Line 52: half digested. Line 55:

compensation. "Twas Silias. Line 56: forred means forward. Line 60: miked. Line 62: broke with. Line 65: land. Line 67: flys. Line 70: appe-tite. This and the following poem, "Laura's Holiday," would seem to be best placed in the "Humorous Poems" section of the typescript.

Laura's Holiday. Line 4: cousin. Line 11: When e're. Line 33: raded. Line 38: wicked". Line 51: was is underlined. Line 52: some one. Line 64: wouldnt. Line 67: need'nt. Line 87: bullets. In the previous stanza one bullet is fired. Line 90: Who ever. Line 113: boyed.

The Chronicles of Sandy Gully as Kept by Skiting Bill. Title: A skite is slang for boaster. Throughout this poem there was very little consistency in the typescript for using an apostrophe to indicate a missing letter at the end of a word. These instances have been silently corrected. Line 1: A pug is a clay mixture used to make bricks. Line 2: would'nt. A shout is when someone is paying for a round of drinks. Line 10: neck.) Paraphrase of line: A scoundrel who knows how to stay ahead of a lynching. Line 12: new-chum. Line 14: fondeled. Line 18: he'ud. Line 19: doctered. Line 20: A toff is an upper-class person. Line 24: A barrer is a barrow. Line 25: susprisin'. Line 26: aggreed. Line 28: thous-and. Line 35: pastys. . . flys. Lines 30 & 36: Coolabis might be a corruption of either Coolgardie or Kalgoorlie gold mines in Australia. Line 34: might'n't. Line 35: pastys. Line 36: Coolabiss. Line 41: fix. Line 44: —Lord. Line 49: O'restless. Line 50: nugged. Line 53: Bil. Line 55: eye glass. Line 65: Expert. Line 67: parry & Bill. Line 68: wan-ted. Line 70: sitten'. Line 72: re-pairs. Line 74: Expert. Published in *Overland Monthly*, Mar. 1908: 298–99. Titled "The 'Te Katipo Extended.' From the Chronicles of Sandy Gully as Kept by Skiting Bill."

A Song of the Hills. Line 13: never resting. Line 17: No indent. Line 18: fued. Line 25: Mt. Tūhua near Lake Kaniere in Westland. Line 27: Achiles . . . un-bending. Line 35: palpating. Line 40: alter. Published in the *Bulletin*, Dec. 13, 1906: 20. This and the three last poems of the typescript are not humorous and do not fit this section.

The Call of the Dream Man. Line 4: way. Line 9: somber. Line 11: abhor-rist. Line 25: wreathe. Line 30: lifes. Published in the *Bulletin*, Jan. 18, 1906: 40; and in the revised *Verses* typescript as "The Scented Garden."

The Last Lover. Line 13: lovéd. Line 21: rythm. Line 38: bridle. Published in the *Bulletin*, Aug. 24, 1905: 3.

The Magic Island. Line 3: concealéd. Line 5. Mer-men. Line 21: chatter-ing. Line 35: follow-ed. Line 40: dip-ping. Line 44: and. Published in the *Bulletin*, Dec. 14, 1905: 26.

quale [kwä-lay]: *Eng.* *n* 1. A property (such as hardness) considered apart from things that have that property. 2. A property that is experienced as distinct from any source it may have in a physical object. *Ital. pron.a.* 1. Which, what. 2. Who. 3. Some. 4. As, just as.